The Book of Revelation and Future Events

The Book of Revelation and Future Events

by

E. W. Rogers

PRECIOUS SEED PUBLICATIONS

© Copyright Precious Seed Publications 2011
The Glebe House, Stanton Drew, Bristol,
UK, BS39 4EH

First published in *Precious Seed* 1970-1971
Reprinted 2011

ISBN: 978 1 871642 41 4

Printed in England

Contents

Page

Preface

Future Events

Our Hope 9
Events in Heaven with the Saints 15
Events on Earth 20
Coming Judgements 24
The Millennium 29
The Consummation 34

The Book of Revelation

Things Which Thou Sawest

Introduction, ch. 1 37

Things Which Are

Introduction, chs. 2-3 43
Ephesus 2. 1-7 46
Smyrna, 2.8-11 49
Pergamos, 2. 12-17 52
Thyatira, 2. 18-29 55
Sardis, 3. 1-6 60
Philadelphia, 3. 7-13 63
Laodicea, 3. 14-22 66

Things Hereafter

A New Scene, chs. 4 71
The Seven Seals, chs. 6, 7 75
Seven Trumpets, ch. 8 79
Three Woes, chs. 9, 10 80

The Two Witnesses, ch. 11 82
The Man Child, ch. 12 84
Two Wild Beasts, ch. 13 87
Six Angels, ch. 14 90
Seven Vials, chs. 15, 16 92
The Great Whore, chs. 17, 18 94
The Grand Finale, chs. 19 to 21. 8. 97
The Bride, the Lamb's Wife, chs. 21. 9 to 22 . . . 100
The End, ch. 22. 6-21. 101

PREFACE

This little book is made up of three parts. The first relates to a series of articles which appeared in *Precious Seed* concerning Future Events. Incorporated in its appropriate place is also a series of articles which appeared in *Precious Seed* touching the seven letters to the churches recorded in the Apocalypse. And the rest of the book is a fresh survey of the book of the Revelation, which does not attempt to go into details but which merely furnishes indications as to what the writer believes to be the only correct way of its interpretation.

It is well-known that there are many differing viewpoints of interpretation of this, the last apocalyptic writing of holy scripture, and that many of the things set forth in these notes are rebutted by ancient and modern interpreters, but the author, after carefully weighing their arguments, remains unconvinced by them. Each one, however, must make up his own mind; he should 'prove all things' by constantly 'examining the scriptures' as the Bereans did, 1 Thess. 5. 21; Acts 17. 11 RV. None should blindly follow a school of thought, or accept teachings because of the names of former men who so taught. Nor, indeed, should any blindly accept what men living today teach. Prestige is no guarantee of accuracy. A Spirit-controlled, unsophisticated faith is all that is requisite to understand what God has written, for the book is not sealed, Rev. 22. 10. Daniel's prophecy was sealed, Dan. 12. 4.

It is the earnest hope of the author and of the publishers that the Spirit of God will use it to the enlightening of the mind and the warming of the heart of God's people, bringing them to one thought, Phil. 2. 2, touching 'things to come'.

E. W. ROGERS

Future Events

OUR HOPE

IN DEALING WITH prophetic matters two dangers should be avoided: (1) that of thoughtlessly following well-known teachers, and (2) that of being altogether silent on the subject. Teachers at the best are but fallible men and, no matter who, his teaching should be subjected to the acid test of 'what saith the scripture?' On the other hand, it would be strange if anyone of the Lord's people were heedless of what the scripture says touching their most precious hope and things which are to follow. Whatever relates to the future glory of our One common Saviour should be of paramount concern to those eternally indebted to Him.

The Unique Place of the Church. In order rightly to understand 'our hope', it is essential to appreciate that 'the church, which is his body', Eph. 1. 22-23, has a unique place in the ways of God. It began on the day of Pentecost, when we were 'all baptized' in the One Spirit 'into one body', 1 Cor. 12. 13 RV, and will be consummated when Christ presents it to Himself 'a glorious church, not having spot, or wrinkle, or any such thing', Eph. 5. 27.

It must not be confused with either (1) the kingdom of God, (2) the family of God, (3) the line of the faithful, or (4) the olive tree testimony, all of which had their beginning long before the church, the body of Christ, came into existence, and all of which will continue for some time – maybe a long time – after the removal of the church at the rapture. The body of Christ should not be equated to any of these. Matthew 8. 11 shows that the kingdom is a comprehensive thing extending over all ages. 1 John 3. 12 shows that the family embraced Abel of long ago, and Abel also heads the list of the 'faithful' in Hebrews 11, while the root of the olive tree clearly goes back to Abraham, Rom. 11.

But the church, the body of Christ, was a 'new' thing altogether – new in kind, Eph. 2. 15. To change the metaphor, Christ Jesus is the chief corner stone of this spiritual temple, of which the apostles and prophets of New Testament times are foundation members, Eph. 2. 20. John the Baptist clearly repudiated the idea that he was the 'bride'; rather, he was 'the friend of the bridegroom', John 3. 29. It follows, therefore, that if he were not part of the bride, then none of his predecessors could have been. In fact, the church was a 'secret' (or a 'mystery') not disclosed to any of the Old Testament prophets, Eph. 3. 5; Col. 1. 26, so it is not found historically or prophetically in the Old Testament. Indeed, in His day the Lord Jesus spoke of it as future, saying 'upon this rock I will build my church', Matt. 16. 18, the words 'will' and 'my' being very significant. It commenced, as we have said, on the day of Pentecost recorded in Acts 2. That event was not repeatable; the church was born then, whence it grew and developed 'unto a perfect man', Eph. 4. 13. The presence of the Spirit of God on earth was essential for the existence of the church, but this could not be until there was the corresponding presence of the risen and glorified Man, Jesus Christ, in heaven. Granted the one, the other necessarily follows; see John 7. 39.

The doctrine of the body of Christ is peculiar to the apostle Paul; no other Bible writer mentions it. Paul learnt it on the Damascus road when he was told that his persecution of the saints was the persecution of Christ; the Head in heaven felt what was done to His members on earth, Acts. 9. 5. It existed before Saul of Tarsus was converted, but it was not formally disclosed to the saints until 'the mystery' had been entrusted to him, Eph. 3. 4, 8.

It must not be imagined, however, that the church was an after-thought with God, that His former ways with man having failed, He tried something else. Rather, the church was the first thing in the mind of God, having been purposed 'before the foundation of the world', Eph. 1. 3-14. Since it was chosen before the foundation of the world, 'times and seasons' have nothing to do with it; its blessings are neither temporal nor earthly, they are eternal and 'in the heavenlies'.

The Rapture. Belonging as the church does to heaven, it is no marvel that Paul discloses another secret, or 'mystery', namely that of the rapture; see 1 Cor. 15. 51ff. and 1 Thess. 4. 13ff. We need not demur at this word *rapture*: it certainly expresses what is taught in scripture, provided that we use the word in the sense (given by the Oxford English Dictionary) of a transportation from one place to another. The reader should examine all the occurrences of the Greek word *harpazo*[1] in the New Testament and he will be left in no doubt as to its significance and the justification of the employment of this one word *rapture* to avoid circumlocution.

The well-known prophecy of Daniel 9 indisputably implies to our mind that there is a long, undefined gap between the 69th week and the 70th. Hippolytus, a bishop of Portus near Rome, one of the most learned of the early fathers at the beginning of the third century, taught this, so the notion is not of late origin. What, then, takes place in the gap? The answer is found in Paul's various 'mysteries', namely (1) the mystery of the calling out of the church, (2) the mystery of the partial and temporary blindness of Israel, Rom. 11. 25, and (3) the mystery of the rapture. Consequent upon Israel's putting to death their Messiah, the nation has been temporarily set on one side. As a train is put into a siding to allow an express train to pass through, after which the train resumes its journey on the line, so Israel has been set aside due to their guilt at Calvary, and the church is now being brought through. When the church is raptured, Israel will again be taken up by God and His dealing on earth will be resumed with the nation. Old Testament histories and ritual all tend to confirm this.

Things that Differ. Before the Lord Jesus left 'his own', John 13. 1, to return to heaven, He assured His followers that He would come again, 14. 3. At times it seems as if He were speaking of His return to earth (as in Matthew 24) and at other times of His return to

---

[1] The word is variously translated: (1) '(to) take by force', Matt. 11. 12; John 6. 15; Acts 23. 10, (2) 'catcheth (away)'. Matt. 13. 19; John 10. 12, (3) 'caught away', Acts 8. 39, (4) '(shall be, or was) caught up', 2 Cor. 12. 2, 4; 1 Thess. 4- 175 Rev. 12. 5, (5) '(to) pluck', John 10. 28, 29, (6) 'pulling', Jude 23.

take them to the Father's house. One thing is clear, that He promised to return visibly and bodily. Acts 1. 11 asserts that 'this Jesus which was received up from you into heaven, shall so come in like manner as ye beheld him going into heaven', RV. His promised return cannot be interpreted as a 'spiritual' return to be fulfilled when the Holy Spirit was sent from heaven. Neither can it allude to death as John 21. 23 makes clear. Zechariah 14. 4 assures us that 'his feet shall stand in that day upon the mount of Olives'.

Until Paul expounded his special teaching, given him by revelation of the Lord, the disciples appear to have expected nothing but the return of the Lord Jesus to earth. They were waiting for Him. But Paul taught them that, when the Lord returns to earth, believers of the present calling will be 'manifested in glory' *with Him*, Col. 3. 4 RV; that God will bring them 'with him', 1 Thess. 4. 14. It is plain, therefore, that if they are to come with Him they must first have gone to be with Him, not all necessarily by death, but those that are living by the rapture. Both the dead in Christ and we that are alive are to be given glorified bodies at the time of the rapture.

It is evident that Paul himself anticipated that the Lord Jesus might come in his lifetime, as shown by the words 'we which are alive and remain', 1 Thess. 4. 17. He identifies himself with the saints living then, but elsewhere he links himself with sleeping believers, 2 Cor. 4. 14. Paul was ready either for the rapture, or for death, or for further service on earth. In like terms he exhorted the saints. The suggestion that Paul had made a mistake, and in his second letter to the Thessalonians wrote correcting the misunderstanding that had been created by his first letter, is to undermine the inerrancy and inspiration of holy scripture. The idea cannot be entertained for a moment.

Nowhere does Paul instruct the saints as to what they should do in preparation for death, nor indeed for any future troublous earthly times. He always encouraged them to wait for Christ – 'till he come' are his words, 1 Cor. 11. 26. This is our distinctive hope. When He comes, sleeping saints will be raised and changed into their glorified bodies; living ones will be changed likewise, and together they will be caught up to meet the Lord in the air, and He will then redeem His promise and take them to the Father's house. His prayer will then have been answered, 'that, where I am they also may be with me', John 17. 24 RV.

All this is in perfect harmony with the Lord's words to Martha, 'he that believeth on me, though he die, yet shall he live: and whosoever liveth and believeth on me shall never die', John 11. 25, 26 RV. But this was not put on record until long after Paul had passed away. Whether Paul knew of this word of the Lord is not clear. Certainly what he wrote to the Thessalonians was 'by the word of the Lord', and was not the product of Paul's wishful thinking. Who, indeed could have imagined such a thing?

The word 'coming', 1 Thess. 4. 15, is the translation of the Greek word *parousia*, a technical word for the return of a person after a period of absence, involving his coming, arrival and resultant stay. The word occurs elsewhere in the New Testament, and the reader should consult a concordance and trace it throughout. Sometimes it relates to an event not connected with the Lord at all; sometimes it is used of His return to earth (see e.g., Matt. 24. 37, 39) and sometimes (as in 1 Thess. 4) it refers to His return to the air. The context of each passage will decide.

Israel's Hope and Ours. Our hope must not be confused with that of Israel. They expect 'the Sun of righteousness', Mal. 4. 2; they look for Him to come to the mount of Olives, Zech. 14. 4. Their horizon is the earth, but our hope is to meet the Lord in the air and to be taken to the Father's house. He will come and receive us; He will descend and we shall ascend and meet Him in the air. The word *meet* need cause no difficulty. Obviously in current usages sometimes two people meet and then part, or they meet and continue on in the direction of either one or the other. The word itself does not imply that the Lord will come to the air, and then continue His journey to earth.

Our hope, 1 Thess. 2. 19, is altogether without indication of date or attendant signs. In Matthew 24 the Lord gave indications of what would happen prior to His return, but these are absent in John

14. 1-3. He did not say when, but left them in a state of constant expectation, though He assured them that, during the time of His absence, they would be hated by the same world that had hated Him, John 16. 1-3.

Paul's teaching follows this same line. No reader of his letters, either then or now, could conclude that Paul told the saints that Christ would not and could not come yet, or that some centuries must ensue before He returned. Let the reader carefully ponder Romans 5. 9; 8. 23; 1 Corinthians 1. 7; 11. 26; 15. 51-57; 2 Corinthians 5. 2; Galatians 5. 5; Philippians 3. 20; Colossians 3. 4; 1 Thessalonians 4. 13-18; 2 Thessalonians 2; 1 Timothy 6. 14; 2 Timothy 4. 8; Titus 2. 13, and he will see that Paul regarded it as an ever-present hope. Acts 20. 29 does not appear to relate to Paul's death but his 'departure' from the Ephesians. Even Peter, who had heard the Lord foretell his (i.e., Peter's) 'decease' (actually, his *exodus*), exhorted the saints to take heed to the prophetic word, not till they died, but 'until the day dawn', 2 Pet. 1. 19.

It is, of course, possible to wait for a person or an event which one knows cannot occur until after certain other things have transpired, but Paul shows in 2 Thessalonians 2 that *before* the apostasy and the manifestation of the man of sin, the *parousia* of the Lord and our gathering together to Him must take place. The whole section should be studied carefully in the Revised Version, the marginal readings being noted particularly.

Have we lost this hope? Has the delay, which is only apparent and not real, caused us to feel some disappointment? Or do earthly things have too great a hold on our affections? Or have we resigned ourselves to the inevitable trouble that must result from the present chaotic conditions? Have we forgotten that 'we shall be saved from (the) wrath through him', Rom. 5. 9, that Jesus is our deliverer from the coming wrath, 1 Thess. 1. 10, and that 'God hath not appointed us to wrath, but to obtain salvation by our Lord Jesus Christ', 1 Thess. 5. 9? We should allow nothing to dim this glorious prospect. May He grant that 'if he shall be manifested, we may have boldness, and not be ashamed before him at his coming (*parousia*)', 1 John 2. 28 RV.

EVENTS IN HEAVEN WITH THE SAINTS

IN THE PREVIOUS CHAPTER we noticed that the rapture is the hope of the church. We are now to consider certain things that are to take place subsequent to this event.

1. The Judgement Seat. It is to be feared that the fact that every believer has to appear before the judgement seat of God does not weigh with us as it should. It is all too easily forgotten, although it forms a large part of the subject of New Testament teaching.

At the time of this event, every believer will have been raised and given his glorified body, so the question of his eternal security is not at all brought into doubt. He is saved on the ground of sovereign grace alone, righteously effected by the death and resurrection of his substitute, Christ Jesus. All his sins have been forgiven, Col. 2. 13; they will never be brought up against him any more, Heb. 10. 17. But his life, work and character will be brought under review, and rewards will be given commensurate therewith. All this will take place when the Lord comes, but not until then.

We are to be Reviewed. This is taught in the three parables that the Lord gave touching (1) the workers in the vineyard, Matt. 20. 1-16, (2) the talents, Matt. 25. 14-30 and (3) the pounds, Luke 19. 11-27. It should be noted that the *principles* of the parables of the virgins and the talents (forming part of the Olivet discourse) apply to us of the present calling as certainly they will apply to the godly after the church is taken out of the way. The Lord will have regard to the inequality of opportunities which His labourers have had, and none will suffer loss because of lack of opportunity and none will have advantage because of large opportunities; this is shown by the parable of the vineyard. Rewards will be strictly commensurate with the work done as the parable of the pounds shows. Ten pounds gained is rewarded by authority over ten cities, and five pounds gained by authority over five cities.

Of course, there are those who assume the place of being the servants of Christ, but in reality are not so. We are not, in this paper, concerned with them. But it must be stated that the security of any true believer is not in jeopardy and no interpretation of either the parable of the talents or the pounds should be such as to undermine this truth.

To be brief, we observe that the parable of the vineyard has regard to *unequal opportunity*, that of the talents to *differing capacities*, and that of the pounds emphasizes a *common responsibility*. The latter two stress the fact that each believer is responsible to the Lord for the trust committed to him, and that he will be examined later, at the time of His return, as to what he has done with it.

Our True Character is to be Revealed. No wonder, then, that in each of the four passages relevant to this subject in the later part of the New Testament the word *each* is to be found. The judgement seat is inescapable for any one of God's people. None need be afraid of it: we shall heartily endorse the decisions made thereat and be glad to see the consumption of all that is worthless, since we can have the utmost confidence in the judgement and estimate of Him who is our Saviour.

In Romans 14. 10, we are told that 'we shall all stand before the judgement-seat of God', RV; moreover, 'each one of us shall give account of himself to God', v. 12 RV. In matters of inconsequential things saints differ each from the other. One can eat anything with an undisturbed conscience; another, who is not altogether free from legalism, is not able to do so. Similarly, in regard to days, and by extension to many other things. Such differences should in no wise engender strife. The one should not 'despise' or 'set at nought' the other, nor should the other condemn the one. Neither is accountable to the other, but each of us shall give an account of himself to God. If God is satisfied with the 'account' or 'reason' that we give for allowing or disallowing anything in our lives, who can say anything otherwise?

'Wherefore judge nothing before the time, until the Lord comes, who will both bring to light the hidden things of darkness, and make manifest the counsels of the hearts; and then shall each man have his praise from God', 1 Cor. 4. 5 RV. Actions will be seen but not motives, and often if the motive were known the action would be differently construed.

'For we must all be made manifest before the judgement-seat of Christ; that each one may receive the things done in the body, according to what he hath done, whether it be good or bad'. This fact should be enough to ensure that 'we make it our aim ... to be well-pleasing unto him', 2 Cor. 5. 9-10 RV. Everything will then come out in its true colours; all the veneer will be stripped off; any concealed cracks will then be exposed. Nothing can be hidden in His presence. We know that 'whatsoever good thing each one doeth, the same shall he receive again from the Lord' no matter his status in life, Eph. 6. 8, and conversely, 'he that doeth wrong shall receive again the wrong that he hath done', Col. 3. 25 RV margin. In these passages the question does not appear to be one of reward but of the revelation of the character we have formed in life. Our actions are like boomerangs, they come back and leave their mark on us. They are as birds on the wing, they take their flight and do their work and then come home to roost. Or, to change the figure, the good things that we have done we may place on the credit side of the ledger of our life: the evil things on the debit side, and the net result is the character that we have formed, its results to be manifest and taken into eternity. How solemn a thought is this! We shall bless God for the blood of Christ that atones for all the wrong: we shall give Him the glory for all the grace given to enable the good things to have been done.

Of course,

Our Actions and Service will be Examined and rewarded appropriately. Of this, 1 Corinthians 3. 1-17 speaks. The passage has to do with work in the local assembly, but its principles apply to all service rendered for the Lord, There were then in the east, as there are today, the magnificent houses of the rich and the hovels of the poor. The one would easily resist fire but the other would readily go up in smoke, its roof being made of grass, straw, or the like. Gold, silver and costly stones (not tiny jewels) will prove incombustible; wood, grass and straw, though bulky, is easily consumable. If our work is such as will resist the fire we shall receive a reward, though such reward will certainly be a token of mercy, 2 Tim. 1. 16, since we are at best 'unprofitable servants', Luke 17. 10. If, however, it is consumed we shall suffer the loss, not of any gift given in sovereign grace, but of a reward which we might otherwise have obtained had we been more diligent. 'He himself shall be saved' is indubitably clear, but how grievous it would be were we to have nothing to show for our redeemed life, nothing that has brought our Redeemer glory and has furthered the work whose foundation He laid by His death. We should be like the servant from whom was taken the one pound that had been given him in trust. He did not share the doom of the enemies, but he had no reward nor further entrusted responsibility in the kingdom, Luke 19. 20ff.

All Faithfulness and Devotion, to be Rewarded. How sad it would be if any of us were to be 'ashamed before him at his coming', 1 John 2. 28. John appears, in this passage, to be thinking of his apostolic labours and the shame that would be brought on him and on the believers were they, at the judgement seat, not to be such as they ought. Both teacher and taught would be ashamed at such poor results. It was to avoid this that Paul exhorted the Philippians to hold forth 'the word of life; that I may have whereof to glory in the day of Christ, that I did not run in vain' and thus fail to receive the reward, 'neither labour in vain', and thus fail to receive his wages, Phil. 2. 16 RV.

Paul was deeply aware that, though in his life he had been wrongly judged not only by the Roman power but also by the saints, yet 'the righteous judge' would, at the *bema*, give to him a victor's crown: he could review his life with humble satisfaction, being conscious of his unswerving loyalty to his Master, 2 Tim. 4. 7-8. Yet he had no exclusive monopoly in this; it was open to all believers as it is open to us today.

The crowned ones are seen in heaven in Revelation 4. 4, and it is pleasing to think that not one believer will then be missing or be without a crown for then shall 'each man have his praise from God', 1 Cor. 4. 5 RV. He will be able to discern what merits such praise, though our eyes fail to detect it.

Not only will the quality of our work come under examination 'of what sort it is', 3. 13, but also the quantity will be taken into consideration, 'how much every man has gained by trading', Luke 19. 15. Nothing will be overlooked, 'whatsoever thou spendest more, when I come again, I will repay thee', 10. 35. 'Behold, I come quickly; and my reward (or wages) is with me, to render to each man according as his work is', Rev. 22. 12 RV and marg. Paul looked forward to that day, and said 'what is our hope, or joy, or crown of rejoicing? Are not even ye in the presence of our Lord Jesus Christ at his coming (*parousia*)?', 1 Thess. 2. 19.

2. The Marriage Supper of the Lamb. There is yet another event to take place before the Lord returns to earth with His people, and that is the marriage supper of the Lamb, Rev. 19. 7ff. In the writer's view there can be no room for doubt that 'the church which is his body' is identical with the bride. We are well aware that this point has been disputed, but it is not uncommon to have one thing viewed in various ways and by sundry metaphors. Ephesians 5. 25ff. confirms the bridal aspect of the church. Besides, in Revelation 19. 9 we read of those who are 'called unto the marriage supper', and we suggest that these guests are the Old Testament saints as well as those gathered in after the rapture, and prior to the coming to earth of the Lord. The bride must not be mistaken for the guests. As the single lady used to be called a 'spinster' because she spun her wedding garments, so too the bride is here seen 'arrayed in fine linen, bright and pure', and we are informed that the 'fine linen is the righteous acts of the saints', Rev. 19. 8 RV. This agrees with what we have already noted touching the manifestation of character. What we do has formed our character, and our clothing signifies that, just as the 'riding habit' is spoken of to denote the equestrian's dress. This clearly is a scene in heaven, as verse 1 states.

There is little wonder that there is so much praise in heaven at this time. The desire of our blessed Lord will then have been fulfilled; His prayer will have been answered, John 17. 24. His heart will be satisfied, for His loved one is with Him.

> He and I, in that bright glory,
> One deep joy shall share –
> Mine, to be for ever with Him;
> His, that I am there.

GERHARDT TERSTEEGEN

EVENTS ON EARTH

WE WILL NOW SET OUT in chronological order, as far as we judge scripture reveals, those things which are to take place on earth after the church has been raptured to heaven.

The Nation of Israel. They are likened to a *vine* when God reviews their *past history*; to an *olive tree*, from which the natural branches have been broken off, when their *present condition* is in view, and to a *fig tree* when their *future prospect* is contemplated. 'Behold the fig tree and all the trees' said the Lord, Luke 21. 29, and He bade His hearers to keep their eye upon them. Certainly today the national life of Israel, as of many other nations, has shown signs of re-appearing. All these nations are like trees, which have long appeared dead, but are now 'shooting forth', a sure indicator that the time of the end is fast drawing near. Events have almost traversed a full circle, and as was to be expected, the Jewish people are once again back in their land, for this is necessary in order that the events of the last times should be fulfilled. When the Lord Jesus was here, there was in Palestine (1) an apostate Jewish people, (2) a dominating Gentile power, and (3) a godly remnant of faithful souls.

So will it be again before He returns. Matthew 10. 23 is one of several passages that seem capable of explanation only on this basis. It should not be forgotten that in the synoptic Gospels (i.e., the first three) the period from the death of Christ until the rapture is passed over in complete silence; the threads of end-time events are taken up from the threads existent when the Lord was here. Jerusalem has been from then until now 'trodden down of the Gentiles' as the Lord foreshadowed, Luke 21. 24. It is not a little significant that the Jewish people are now back in Palestine under the autonomous state called 'Israel', though they are somewhat dependent upon the protective care of the western powers against their eastern and northern enemies. Surely events are taking place before our eyes which show that the stage is being rapidly prepared for the last great drama of earth before the Lord returns in power.

The Roman Empire. Another fact which the scriptures make plain, as the present writer believes, is the resuscitation of the former Roman empire. The beast that was, is not, and shall be, Rev. 17. 8, alludes to this, the word 'beast' being used in the Apocalypse both of the empire and of its head. This agrees with the ten toes of the image in Daniel 2, with the ten horns of the beast in Daniel 7, and with the re-appearance of the four beasts of that chapter, identical with the first 'beast' in Revelation 13. 1ff. The capital of this revived empire and the seat of its head will be Rome; see Rev. 17. 18. The fact that the ancient Roman law is the basis of modern jurisprudence, and the further fact that the proposed Common Market is based on the Treaty of Rome is not without significance, though we must not be ensnared into playing the role of prophets. But the wise shall understand.

Christendom. God will judicially send a 'strong delusion' over those who have rejected the gospel they heard, 2 Thess. 2. 10-12. The apostasy will then be in full-bloom, and everything basically Christian will be denied, 2. 3. Religiously, Christendom will have become 'the great harlot', Rev. 17. 1 RV, Satan's counterfeit of the true bride of Christ. The reader should ponder carefully Revelation 17, comparing it with the past history of the corrupt church of Rome and with the present frantic endeavours by both Roman and Protestant ecumenical councils to secure a unified 'church'. It is 'drunken with the blood of the saints', for it is, and will yet again prove itself to be, the relentless enemy of God and of His people. At the present moment there is a Hinderer and a hindrance, 2 Thess. 2. 7, 6, to the full development of this unification of Christendom. The Spirit of God, the Hinderer, in the church, the hindrance, is restraining things intentionally, purposefully and intelligently with the view that the head of this corrupt system shall not become manifest till his proper time. Though various suggestions have been made as to this Hinderer, yet the only one that seems to satisfy all the requirements is that here given. No system of government, no principle of rule, no earthly ruler could so control and restrain events that the Man of sin should not appear until 'his own season'.

Consequent upon the removal of the church and of the Spirit of God in the church, there will be

Chaotic Conditions on Earth. Not that we are to suppose that the Spirit of God will no longer operate on earth. Rather He will resume the method adopted in Old Testament times; He will work on earth from heaven. Further, there will be godly souls who will refuse to participate in the unified godless 'church' then formed, and they will in consequence suffer. But of that anon.

Things on earth will be much like they were in the days of Noah and of Lot (see Luke 17. 26, 28). Business will proceed as usual; life will seem very ordinary, save that the times will be marked by 'violence and corruption' (see Gen. 6). And if this is so today, whatever will it be when the 'salt of the earth' has been removed! It will be like to the cities of Sodom and Gomorrah, where the name of one of these cities gives us a word for the grossest of moral iniquity. Do we lament the dreadful downward trend of things in our times? Let us remember, the Lord's *parousia* is at the door, but do not let us be deceived into supposing that the world will become better. Nothing but divine judgement will cleanse the earth; the flood of Noah's day and the fire of Lot's day declare this eloquently.

There will be at the end times be

Two Prominent Persons, the one at the head of the revived Roman empire and the other at the head of the apostate Jewish people. The first beast of Revelation 13 will be the *political* leader of the then Roman earth, and the other the head of the unified system of *religion* which will be utterly Christless and godless. There will be a caricature of the Holy Trinity, for instead of the True, there will be the head of the empire appropriating to himself divine claims. Subordinate to him will be the second beast of Revelation 13 whose prime work will be to secure worship to the first beast by all on earth, and behind each will be the unseen dragon, the devil. 'I am come in my Father's name, and ye receive me not: if another shall come in his own name, him ye will receive', John 5. 43. That 'another' will then have come. He will be the 'idol shepherd', Zech. 11. 17; the wilful king, Dan. 11. 36; the 'man of lawlessness', 2 Thess. 2. 3 RV marg. His seat will be in Jerusalem, where presumably the temple will have been rebuilt and in which he will place 'the abomination of desolation (that maketh desolate)', Matt. 24. 15. As ever, politics and religion will go hand in hand; the woman rides the beast.

Seven Year Covenant. Daniel 9. 27 speaks of a covenant which the coming prince (the first beast of Revelation 13) will make with the mass of the Jewish people. Isaiah 28. 15 reveals it to be a defensive pact, with a view to safeguarding the Jewish state from the inroads of the powers north and east of them. It will be made for a term of seven years (i.e., one week – the last week of Daniel 9. 24). Space does not permit us to go into this key prophecy in detail, though it should be remarked that a proper understanding of this will provide a clue as to the correct interpretation of the bulk of the prophetic scriptures. The writer may be permitted to refer to his book *Concerning the Future*, in which this prophecy is treated fully.

Many scriptures show that the pact will be ineffective in achieving its military purpose. The reader should study Zechariah 14. 1-3; Revelation 14. 9-20; 16. 13-16; Isaiah chapters 2-10, amongst many others.

COMING JUDGEMENTS

AS WE HAVE BEEN REVIEWING the development of things on earth, doubtless men both now and then forget that there is One in the heavens. For long He has kept silence, but in His own time He will break that silence. 'I have long time holden my peace'. He says, 'I have been still, and refrained myself: now will I cry', Isa. 42. 14. 'I will go and return to my place, till they (Israel) acknowledge their offence, and seek my face', Hosea 5. 15. But we now have to consider how He breaks His silence.

War in Heaven. The first step is the casting out of heaven of one who is variously described as 'the dragon', 'the great dragon', 'that old serpent', 'the devil', 'Satan', 'the deceiver of the whole world', 'the accuser of our brethren'.

We shall not describe the history of that fallen created dignitary, nor of the hosts that followed him. But the reader should carefully study Revelation 12. 7ff. Indeed, the whole of the chapter should be studied for it speaks of events both on earth and in heaven that precipitate the 'great tribulation'. The woman which brought forth the man child is the nation of Israel 'of whom as concerning the flesh Christ came', Rom. 9. 5. The 'casting down' of the devil occurs in the middle of Daniel's prophetic last week, Dan. 9. 24ff., so that 'for a time, and times and half a time', for 'twelve hundred and sixty days', for three and a half years, the Jewish people are made the particular butt of the enemy's venom. The reader should refer to Isa. 10. 22; 28. 15; 8. 7-8; 59. 19, throwing light on the serpent's casting 'out of his mouth water as a flood after the woman, that he might cause her to be carried away of the flood', Rev. 12. 15. By comparing scripture with scripture, much light is thrown on what at first appears to be obscure.

All this is confirmed by the threefold occurrence of the word 'wrath' in 1 Thessalonians. It is that wrath spoken of in Romans 5. 9; Revelation 6. 16, 17; 11. 18; 14. 10; 16. 19; 19. 15. Jesus is our

Deliverer from it, 1 Thess. 1. 10; God has not appointed us to it, 5. 9; the Jews are the special object of it, consequent upon their rejection of their true Messiah, 2. 16. Yet, as we might expect, in those terrible days God has special regard for His faithful remnant. He provides a place for them, Rev. 12. 14; His 'pavilion' is always available to them, and He causes even nature itself to come to their aid.

If the reader goes carefully through the book of Revelation and notes what it says concerning what transpires 'in', 'from' and 'out of' heaven, he will readily be able to glean those things which occur there after the rapture and before the Lord actually comes to earth.

The Great Tribulation. In the middle of the last week of 'the times of the Gentiles', the head of the Roman empire with whom the covenant was made will not, as is commonly asserted, break the covenant, but will deprive the Jewish people of their religious liberty and an idolatrous system will be set up in its stead. Daniel 3. 2; 2 Thessalonians 2. 4 and Revelation 13. 14 all shed light on this. An image will be set up in the temple at Jerusalem and, should any one refuse to bow to the image, or should they worship any other god, their punishment will be of like severity to that of the three godly men in the heated furnace and Daniel in the den of lions.

The whole of Revelation 12 relates primarily to the last half of the last week of Daniel's prophecy. It is 'in the midst of the week he shall cause the sacrifice and the oblation to cease', Dan. 9. 27, and in its stead he will set up the 'image' which represents the deification of the political head of the revived Roman empire, to which image everyone will be required to give worship. That this passage relates to the same period as that mentioned in Revelation 12 seems clear from the fact that the half of 'the week' is 3½ years, 1,260 days, 42 months, 'a time, and times and half a time'. It will be a time of trouble unequalled at any time in the world's history. If the reader will consult Daniel 12. 1; Joel 2. 2; Jeremiah 30. 7; and Matthew 24. 21 he will see that all the passages refer to the one period, since there cannot be more than one period the like of which has never been before nor shall ever be again.

It is the time of 'the tribulation, the great one' as Revelation 7. 14 reads literally. Throughout the whole of human history the godly have always known 'tribulation' from the hand of the ungodly, but none has ever been like that which is yet to come. It will be Jacob's trouble – the time when God will take that nation at their word when they said 'His blood be on us, and on our children', Matt. 27. 25. Divine wrath has come upon them to the uttermost, 1 Thess. 2. 16. The crime at Calvary has yet to be avenged on those who will not repent.

It will be terminated by the coming to earth of the Lord Jesus, delivering the persecuted godly remnant who have been waiting for Him, and inflicting judgement on His and their foes. He that endures to the end of that time will be saved bodily by the active intervention of the Lord from heaven. Were it not so, were those days not thus delimited and shortened, no flesh would be saved. For note carefully, it is here a question of the salvation not of the soul but of the body – the 'flesh'; (see Matt. 24. 22).

The Lord's Return in Judgement and Glory. Then 'they shall see the Son of man coming in the clouds of heaven with power and great glory'. Matt. 24. 30. So spake the Lord concerning His return to earth. Oftentimes, one word of scripture becomes the key with which to unlock its secrets, and this is the case with the word *until*. It is found in Matthew 22. 44, 'Sit thou on my right hand, *till* I make thine enemies thy footstool'. When the Lord returns to earth, it will inaugurate the period of His reign which will be unbroken '*till* he hath put all enemies under his feet', 1 Cor. 15. 25. He will then present, though not relinquish, the kingdom in a subjugated state to 'God, even the Father'.

Again in Matthew 23. 39 we read, 'Ye shall not see me henceforth, *till* ye shall say, Blessed is he that cometh in the name of the Lord'. For when the Lord returns to earth the nation of Israel will have gone through the furnace of affliction, and their heart will turn to the Lord. Meanwhile, 'Jerusalem shall be trodden down of the Gentiles, *until* the times of the Gentiles be fulfilled', Luke 21. 24. At the same time it is said of the Lord that 'the heaven must receive

(Him) *until* the times of restitution of all things', Acts 3. 21. He is in heaven, whilst of the nation to which He first came it is said 'blindness in part is happened to Israel, *until* the fulness of the Gentiles be come in', Rom. 11. 25. So that 'even *unto* this day, when Moses is read, the vail is upon their heart. Nevertheless when it (their hearts) shall turn to the Lord, the vail shall be taken away', 2 Cor. 3. 15-16.

From these passages, we learn that the return to earth of the Lord Jesus will have effects upon the nation of Israel and upon their capital city Jerusalem, as well as upon the world at large. God does not intend that His Son should remain unvindicated in the world where He was so grossly dishonoured. He decrees that the very city that cast Him out will be that which will let Him in, Psalm 24. The very people who said 'We will not have this man to reign over us' will say 'Lo, this is our God; we have waited for him', Isa. 25. 9.

The writer may refer the reader to his book *Jesus the Christ* wherein is discussed the Olivet discourse of the Lord given in Matthew 24. This discourse relates to the return to earth of the Lord Jesus and nowhere is there to be found in it any reference to the rapture. Although verse 14 has been referred to the present-day aspect of the gospel, yet as a matter of fact it refers to what is there called 'this gospel of the kingdom', a term defined in the preceding verse 13. It has to do with bodily salvation, not that of the soul (cp. v. 22), to be realized when the Lord comes. Of course, all aspects of God's good news for men are based on the cross, whether prospectively or retrospectively, but the word 'gospel' merely means good news. The particular kind of good news implied must be understood from any other words attached to the word 'gospel'. It will always be true that blessing can only come by faith in Christ, but verse 13 presupposes that. In this present day, we are waiting for the Lord who shall change our bodies of humiliation and fashion them like unto His body of glory. Our citizenship is in heaven, Phil. 3. 20, 21; but those to whom Matthew 24 refers will be waiting for the Lord to come to earth.

Important Differences. Further, verses 40 and 41 have been construed, as we judge entirely wrongly, as relating to the rapture. But the very reverse of what occurs at the rapture is the case. Then 'one shall be taken' in judgement 'and the other left' for blessing, the blessing of the millennial kingdom. This contrasts with the rapture, when one is taken away for blessing and the other is left for judgement. That this interpretation of the verse is sound is proved in the context by the citation of Noah and the flood, when 'the flood came, and took them all away' in judgement while Noah and his family were left for blessings on the then new earth, Matt. 24. 37-39.

The contrast with the rapture is very marked. Here in Matthew 24 there is no mention of any resurrection; the Lord comes to people living on earth. But at the rapture, which takes place earlier, sleeping saints will be raised. Here in Matthew 24 there are both sign-marks and time marks, but none is given for the rapture. In the Upper Room, the Lord did not say anything about 'one this and another that'. They were wholly one company, not to be divided when He comes. At the rapture there is no discrimination, but there will be at the coming to earth with which Matthew 24 deals. In this Olivet discourse, the Lord speaks of Himself as the Son of man, a title which, when used prophetically, implies judgement. But that title is not used in John 14; in the Upper Room the Lord uses pronouns in the first person, but in the Olivet discourse He speaks in the third person.

The First and the Second Advent to Earth. When the Lord first came to earth it was in humiliation and in poverty. When He comes next it will be in power and great glory. At His incarnation a multitude of the heavenly host expressed His praises. But 'when he (God) again bringeth in the firstborn into the world (inhabited earth)', that is, His beloved Son, '*all* the angels of God' will worship Him, Heb. 1. 6 RV and marg. For God has resolved that the One who had a cross outside Jerusalem shall yet have a throne inside the city. The crucified 'King of the Jews' shall yet reign on earth as King of kings and Lord of lords. The people who once rejected Him will then, as a purged and regenerate nation, welcome Him.

The Final Clash. 'The kings of the east', Rev. 16. 12, and the 'king of the north' and the 'king of the south', Dan. 11. 40, will with others all make their attack on God's earthly people and on His land. This will necessitate that the Roman power, having made a military pact with Israel, will consequently be brought into the conflict. Zechariah 14. 2 shows that the attacks will result in terrible distress, but the victory is assured as verse 4 of that chapter indicates. All the details do not appear to be made plain, though doubtless at the time of fulfilment all will be clear. But the two beasts of Revelation 13 – 'the beast' and 'the false prophet' will be sent alive, body and soul, direct into the lake of fire, Rev. 19. 20. There will be no intermediate state in Hades for them. Such psalms as Psalm 46 will be particularly appropriate at such a time as this. At the same time, we recognize that many prophecies that relate to this victory also have a historical background, since past events adumbrate the future and ultimate triumph of the Lord. Therefore many prophecies may be read historically and prophetically. When read historically, it should always be borne in mind that that does not exhaust their implications.

THE MILLENNIUM

IT IS STRANGE that, although the phrase a 'thousand years' occurs six times in Revelation 20. 1-7, there are those who deny that there is to be any such time to come. We do not understand how this conclusion is reached. Most surely the devil is not bound now; he is very much active. Those who deny the millennium appear to have insuperable difficulty in this section.

There is such a time of peace to come, following on the Lord coming out of heaven, and 'triumphing gloriously', delivering His godly earthly people and destroying Gentile civilisation. He will prove to be the stone 'cut out of the mountain without hands' of which Daniel spoke in chapter 2 of his book. The longed-for boon of worldwide peace will then be realized and the intolerable burden of arms accumulation will have gone; see Psalm 72; Isa. 2. 4; 9. 7.

Before going into details, we may remark that such passages as Isaiah 11; 35; 65. 17ff. all speak of this time. The 'whole creation', which today 'groaneth and travaileth in pain together', 'waiteth for the manifestation of the sons of God', issuing in the creation being 'delivered from the bondage of corruption' under which it now lies; see Rom. 8. 19ff. The passages in Isaiah should not be read as mere picture-language or poetry with no substantial reality behind them. The fact is that the curse of the fall will then have been removed, and conditions will be similar to, though better than, those prior to Adam's fall. With the return of the Lord Jesus to earth, there will be global disturbances such as are spoken of in Zechariah 14. 3ff. and Ezekiel 47. 6ff., for whatever spiritual lessons these chapters have (and they have many), their literal significance cannot and should not be dismissed. The geographical changes which are to take place in the area of the Dead Sea are such as will make Jerusalem a political centre, a position that it has never before enjoyed, not even in the heyday of its history.

Opening Features. This kingdom will be introduced with *judgement*, just as was the case with Solomon's kingdom; see 1 Kings 1-3. This judgement is spoken of in Matthew 25. 31ff. and must not be confused with the judgement of the Great White Throne. It is a mistake to group all the various future judgements together, as if there were to be one final assize. We have already spoken of the judgement of sin when Christ died on the cross. Then there is judgement which 'must begin at the house of God' and that goes on today; see 1 Cor. 11. 32. Later there is to be the judgement seat, of which we have already spoken in this series. That will take place in heaven, prior to the return of the Lord to earth. But now we are thinking of the judgement that He will introduce when He comes back to earth. Matthew 25. 34 clearly shows it takes place at the commencement of the millennial kingdom, into which the blessed are to enter. It is a judgement on earth, and will have as its criterion the manner in which persons have acted towards the brethren of the

Lord. These as we have seen are chiefly, though not exclusively, the faithful Jewish remnant who will witness during the last unequalled troublous times. This assize differs from that of the Great White Throne in its time, in its place, in its criterion, and in its procedure. Moreover there is no resurrection in Matthew 25. 32; these are persons living on earth at that time.

At the commencement of this millennial kingdom the Lord will take steps to regather the scattered of Israel, to bring them back to their land, and to re-unite the divided ten and two tribes, unifying them as one nation over which He will be their King. We ask the reader to read Ezekiel 37 and to say whether or not this is not its plain meaning. The wise words of HOOKER come to mind at this point, applying to Ezekiel 37 and other passages:

'I hold it for a most infallible rule in exposition of sacred scripture that where a literal construction will stand, the farthest from the letter is commonly the worst. There is nothing more dangerous than this licentious and deluding art which changeth the meaning of words as alchemy doth or would do the substance of metals, making of anything what it listeth and bringeth in the end all truth to nothing'.

Blissful Characteristics. The wildness of the beasts is one product of Adam's fall. The crown of authority fell from his head, but when the 'last Adam', 'the Lord from heaven' shall assume His rights as 'Son of man' on earth, then the 'wolf also shall dwell with the lamb, and the leopard shall lie down with the kid; and the calf and the young lion and the fatling together; and a little child shall lead them', Isa. 11. 6.

Whatever spiritual lessons may be gleaned from this chapter (and 'whatsoever things were written aforetime were written for our learning'), do not allow such applications to nullify the plain meaning of the passage. The passage tells of the character of the King, the beneficent effects of His presence on the animal kingdom, the recovery of the nation of Israel after their age-long dispersal, and even the transformation of the delta of the Nile, v. 15.

It seems that life will be prolonged to that which obtained in the days of the patriarchs. If a child should die, being reckoned but a child when one hundred years old, what shall be said of man? The best way to know what the millennium will be like is to read the relevant passages. Isaiah 65. 17ff. is one such. The state of Israel may be flourishing today but it is destined for God's ultimate judgement. Yet God's eye is and ever has been on 'the pleasant land', 'a land flowing with milk and honey' and He intends to redeem His promise and give it to Abraham and his seed, free from the foot of the invader, and in the condition in which Abraham looked for it, for he desired 'a better country, that is, an heavenly', namely not heavenly in location but in condition.

The whole of the area surrounding Palestine is to undergo a change. Ezekiel 37 is not the only passage bearing on this. Zechariah 14. 4ff. speaks of it. The 'living waters' of verse 8 mean just what is said, else what can be made of the 'former sea' and the 'hinder sea'? This, coupled with the healing of the Dead Sea, and the earthquake, v. 4, shows that the Middle East is to be the scene not only of terrible war, but frightening seismic disturbances.

God's Promises Realized. Jerusalem will become, in fact, the 'city of the great King' and all nations which are left for the millennial kingdom will send their delegates annually to worship the King of kings and the Lord of lords, 'the King, the Lord of hosts'; see Zech. 14. 16. It will be the great centre to which 'all nations shall flow' in order that they may be taught the ways of the God of Jacob, so that they may walk in His paths, Isa. 2. 2-3. The twelve apostles will have administrative authority over the twelve tribes of Israel, Luke 22. 30. The King will be seen then, not as 'a man of sorrows, and acquainted with grief' whose 'visage was so marred more than any man', but as the 'King in his beauty', Isa. 33. 17. To this Psalm 45 refers. In that kingdom the believer of the present calling will 'reign with him (Christ)', 2 Tim. 2. 12.

God magnifies His word above all the honours of His name, and unconditional covenants made by Him will be fulfilled. Hence the covenant made to Abram, so specific in Genesis 15. 18-21, is sure to be literally fulfilled. This defies spiritualizing, and Ezekiel's vision of the division of the land throws much light on what God will do in implementing His word, Ezek. 48. Similarly in David's case; God assured him 'thy throne shall be established for ever'; see Psalm 89. 34-37. It is true that everything is both to be realized in, and to be effected by Christ risen from the dead, but the future fulfilment of God's promise is certain; God 'cannot lie', Titus 1. 2.

Israel's Place in the World. Owing to Israel having broken the word of the Lord, they have long been the 'tail' of all nations. But later, when God has purged and renewed them, they will again be the 'head' as envisaged in Deuteronomy 28. 13. They will then be the dominant world-power under the rule of their Messiah. The nation, though apparently long since dead, will be brought to life again (see Dan. 12. 2; Ezek. 37), and their teachers will turn many to righteousness, Dan. 12. 3 marg. The writer cannot regard Ezekiel's vision from chapter 40 onwards as anything else but that yet to be literally fulfilled. It is not proper to spiritualize one part and read literally another part. Consequently, it would appear that the Dead Sea is to be healed; the land in its full promised extent is to be apportioned out to the tribes of Israel; the temple is to be built with significant differences from Solomon's temple; the sacrifices are to be resumed commemoratively as before they were anticipative. Then will have come to pass the full significance of the feast of tabernacles, 'Every man shall dwell under his own vine and under his own fig tree'. Spiritually, politically, socially, and economically He who was born of Mary, but whose goings forth have been from of old, from eternity, will do what none other has ever been able to do – He will put things right on earth for the glory of God and the good of man.

What of the church in that day? Then 'the saints shall judge the world'; 'we shall judge angels', 1 Cor. 6. 2-3. Just as now the administration of earth's affairs is in the hands of principalities and powers (see Daniel 10) so then, under Christ, it will be in the hands of the saints, who will reign over the earth, Rev. 5. 10.

THE CONSUMMATION

IT MUST NOT BE SUPPOSED that the millennium will be a perfect state. There will be

A Further Rebellion. Some of its subjects will yield only feigned obedience. Rebellion there will be, but it will be visited by summary punishment; see Psalm 18. 44 marg.; Isa. 65. 20. The millennium, as a matter of fact, is God's final test of man. Man will then no longer be able to blame the devil for his wrongs, for the devil will have been incarcerated for one thousand years in the abyss. Nor will man be able to blame the system of rule, since he will have for that long period an inflexibly righteous King, Isa. 32. 1. But it will reveal that 'that which is born of flesh is flesh' and is incurable under the best circumstances. So that at the end, when Satan is released, mankind will flock to his standard and rebel against the best King that the earth will ever have had. But the rebellion will be short-lived, and conclude disastrously for the rebels; see Rev. 20. 7-10.

The Dissolution of Heaven and Earth. We read 'the earth and the heaven fled away', Rev. 20. 11, which is the seer's way of expressing what Peter describes at greater length in 2 Peter 3. The hands that 'hold together' creation now, Col. 1. 17 RV marg., will then release the hold and the elements will become disintegrated. The elements will 'melt' and 'be dissolved', two English words representing but one Greek word and implying the unloosing of the bond that holds all together now. The globe is stored with fire, but this is restrained until the restraint is removed when the works of the earth will be burned up. This disintegration of the elements will result in a new heaven and a new earth, wherein righteousness will make its permanent abode. In the millennium, righteousness will reign, but there will be factors which will call for repression; no such contrary elements will exist in the eternal state. It is the writer's view that Revelation 21. 1-8 describes the eternal state, while the remainder of the chapter describes millennial conditions.

The Great White Throne. We do not need to repeat our warning that the various judgements should not be confused one with the other. The Great White Throne is the final judgement. Revelation 20. 11-13 describes this dreadful scene which should be pondered on one's knees. God save us from speaking of it without anguish of heart for the lost. It is subsequent to the intermediate state described in Luke 16. 19-31. All the lost in that state are here raised in their bodies to be cast 'soul and body into Gehenna', Matt. 10. 28 RV marg. Mark 9. 48 presents dreadful words, but these were uttered by Him who died that none might perish. We must beware lest we construe the word 'perish' wrongly. It does not mean annihilation. Reference to the consistent usage of this word in the New Testament will satisfy anyone as to that. Besides, in English we do not imply annihilation when we say that a thing has perished; we mean that it is no longer serviceable for its original purpose.

John 5. 24 is a general statement, applicable to all who put their faith in the Lord Jesus, thus assuring them of absolute exemption from appearance at the Great White Throne. They may have boldness at that time, for 'as he (the Lord Jesus) is, so are we in this world', 1 John 4. 17. He is on the other side of judgement which is eternally past for Him, and for us also who are in Christ. The enemy of God and man now has his agents who appear as 'angels of light' and, by plausible arguments and pathetic appeals, alleging acquaintance with the original languages, seek to deceive people into believing that the punishment of the Christ-rejecter is not 'eternal'. We cannot occupy space in rebutting such arguments but, suffice it to say, that if the word is admittedly 'eternal' as to 'eternal life', then it certainly is so as to 'eternal punishment'; see Matthew 25. 46 RV, and all other places where the word is found in the New Testament.

If these lines should be read by any one not yet saved, let him remember 'now is the accepted time; behold, now is the day of salvation', 2 Cor. 6. 2. It is too late after death.

The Eternal State. The grandeur of this can only be described in terms that are understood on earth, so that we may apprehend in but a small way, based on our present limited experience, the marvellous joys that await the redeemed. There will be no more death, nor tears, nor sorrow, nor crying, nor pain. Let the reader examine Revelation 21. 7-8 and enquire in his heart in which class he is, for there are only two – the sons of verse 7 or the lost of verse 8. There is no neutral ground.

Finale. The writer is only too aware that almost at every turn nowadays the things here presented are either challenged or denied. We have not dealt with the several objections raised by those who are not enemies of the truth but who are honestly perplexed. We can only invite our readers to remember the words of Paul to the recently converted Thessalonians; 'despise not prophesyings; prove all things; hold fast that which is good; abstain from every form of evil', 1 Thess. 5. 20-22 RV. And again, 'Consider what I say; and the Lord give thee understanding in all things', 2 Tim. 2. 7.

In reading the prophetic scriptures, we should endeavour to approach them, as far as we can, free from all preconceived ideas. Present teachers are not infallible and so we should test all that which we have been taught. Even the Bereans tested what Paul taught in the light of scripture, and we have no Pauls today. The writer may refer the reader to his book *Concerning the Future* in which a chapter is devoted to the interpretation of prophecy. It may help in the further pursuance of this entrancing topic.

The Book of Revelation

Things Which Thou Sawest

INTRODUCTION

REVELATION 1

THE FIRST THREE VERSES of chapter 1 are introductory to the whole book. It is the unveiling of a Person at present hidden from the eyes of men in the glory of heaven but who soon ('shortly'), and inevitably ('must') will be manifested in glory on earth. The transmission of this 'revelation' or *unveiling* is not direct, but God gave it to the Lord Jesus, and He in turn sent it by the angel to his bondservant John, who in turn conveyed it to the churches, and to all who would read (publicly), hear and keep the words of the prophecy which he wrote. This is because things are so disordered on earth that God can make no direct approach.

What John wrote is the 'word of God' and its subject is 'the testimony of Jesus Christ', that is, 'the testimony of (given to) Jesus is the spirit of prophecy', Rev. 19. 10. There is a special blessing, happiness or joy for those who publicly read, and those who submissively hear (i.e. obey) and keep what is herein written. If the time was 'near' then, how much nearer must it be today!

The book is full of symbols, for the Lord Jesus 'sent and signified' it by the angel. Not that everything herein is symbolic. The reader must discriminate between what is literal and what is figurative.

In verses 4 to 7 John addresses himself to the seven churches of Asia. He conveys a message from all three Persons of the Holy Trinity. 'Him which is, and which was, and which is to come' 'refers to God the Father in the eternity of His being: the Jehovah, the great 'I am' of the Old Testament, the Eternal One. 'The seven Spirits which are before his throne' refers to the One Holy Spirit in the perfection of His activities as the numeral seven implies. Read Isaiah 11. 2 for the enumeration of these seven things. 'And from Jesus Christ' – seven things are predicated of Him as follows:

1. The faithful witness,
2. The firstborn of the dead,
3. The ruler of the kings of the earth,
4. He loveth us,
5. He washed us in His blood,
6. He made us a kingdom, priests unto His God and Father,
7. Behold He cometh with clouds.

The doxology at the end of verse 6 is not omitted in order to invent a series of seven. It is the outburst of John's heart as he reviews what the Lord Jesus now *is*, as compared with what he knew of Him in the days of His flesh. *Then* He was 'a man of sorrows, and acquainted with grief'; *then* He was 'despised and rejected of men' but *now* He is crowned as a victor 'with glory and honour'. *Then* He was crucified in weakness, 2 Cor. 13. 4, but *now* He has what the KJV and RV calls 'dominion'; the word John uses denotes might, strength, power. And although His dishonour and weakness lasted but for a little time, the glory and dominion are His for ever and ever. Who, then, can fail to add their Amen to this, not so much as an expression of a wish but as the affirmation of a fact (as, indeed, the word 'Amen' means).

But as to the seven items, it will be observed that John had a tidy mind, for although the scriptures are God-breathed, God utilized the special traits of His penman to His own ends. John does not enumerate these seven items haphazardly but each is placed in its right position. The *central item*, the fourth of the series, is, He 'loveth us', RV. It is the timeless participle telling of His everlasting love. It is the cause which explains every one of the other six items. Let the reader put the question *Why?* to each of these six items, and he will find the true answer in every case to be His ceaseless love for us. We do not amplify this but leave the reader to do this for himself.

Further, the first three items are *personal* to the Lord irrespective of other persons; they refer to what He is in Himself. But

38

the last three items are *relative*, namely, what He has done, or will do for others. He washed us, He made us, and every eye shall see Him. We should never fail to think first of the essential glories of our Lord before we consider His relative ones. We are so apt to reverse this order and to put our benefits first.

Again, items 1, 2 and 3 relate respectively to the *past, present* and *future* in that order, and similarly the last three items are placed in the same arrangement.

He *was*, when on earth, the outstanding and unfailing faithful Witness. All other witnesses were faulty in some respect. How unflinchingly He bore witness to the truth! He *is* now in heaven, the firstborn of the dead, a surety that His people will follow in due course. And He *will yet be* manifestly the ruler of all the kings of the earth – not merely ten of them as the Man of sin will be.

So, too, with the last three. He 'washed us from our sins in his own blood', or as the R.V. has it, 'loosed us'. The difference is only that of one Greek letter in the original, yet it little matters. We are redeemed by 'precious blood', 1 Pet. 1. 19, and that agrees with loosing. 'The blood of Jesus Christ . . . cleanseth us from all sin', 1 John 1. 7, and that agrees with washing.

> He breaks the power of cancelled sin,
> And sets the prisoner free;

that agrees with loosing;

> His blood can make the foulest clean,
> His blood avails for me;

that agrees with washing. All this is in the *past*.

But in the *present* He has made us a kingdom, priests unto God and His Father. Every believer is in His kingdom, and every believer is a priest. This is not the place to dilate on the common priesthood of all believers, men and women alike. There is now no such thing as a selective priesthood whatever may have obtained in the times of Israel. Nor has priesthood anything to do with spiritual attainment.

The enjoyment and exercise of its privileges certainly have to do with that, but the position is that of every believer through sovereign grace. Naturally it involves responsibilities but of these we cannot now speak particularly. Nor should priesthood be confused with ministry, namely service in and to the church. Each is different.

Furthermore, He will soon come with clouds, emblematic of the glory of the divine presence, and He will be seen by all, particularly by His earthly people Israel who were primarily responsible for His death. 'All the tribes of the earth', RV, or better 'the land', shall mourn over Him. Isaiah 53 will then be the national confessional lament of Israel when the days of Zechariah 12. 10-14 are come. The whole world waits on Israel's repentance of their guilt of murdering their Messiah. When that occurs, the door will be open for universal Gentile and earthly blessing.

It is not easy to affirm who is the speaker in verse 8, but if, as seems likely, it is the Lord Jesus, then it is an incidental evidence of the absolute equality in every respect of the Persons of the Godhead, each with the other, cp. v. 4. He is the sum total of all divine revelation, as the first and the last letters of the Greek alphabet, Alpha and Omega, imply. He is beyond the limits of all time, and there is nothing outside of His power – He is Almighty.

Perhaps at this point we should consider verse 19 wherein there is indicated **the threefold division of the book**. 'The things which thou sawest', RV, refer plainly to chapter 1; note vv. 10, 12, 17. 'The things which are' relate to the seven churches that were then existent and whose character and history were symbolically instructive. 'The things which shall come to pass hereafter', RV, refers to what is contained in chapter 4 onwards. Those who read their Greek Testament cannot fail to observe the identity of the phrases used in each case in 1. 19 and 4. 1. Nothing, it would seem, could be plainer. This interpretation is neither forced nor the product of wishful thinking.

If, as we have no doubt, this is correct, then plainly what John saw is defined in chapter 1. Chapters 2 and 3 define conditions ecclesiastically as they then were and as they have persisted until the present time, and chapter 4 onwards shows what will yet transpire in the not distant future.

We are aware that attempts have been made to amend the translation of 1. 19, but the KJV, RV, RSV, and NEB all concur. Therefore we accept this translation without further question.

The word 'hereafter', or the fuller phrase 'after these things', must not be construed to read as if it said to John, 'After you have seen these things', as has been suggested. That is not what is written. If there appears to be a parallel between what has now gone into history and what is symbolized or affirmed in chapter 4 onwards of this Apocalypse, it is merely because the same evil principles yield the same results: past events may be but precursors of what is yet to be fully developed and consummated.

'The Things which thou Sawest.' John's *relationship* is that of 'your brother'. His *circumstances* are 'partaker with you in the tribulation and kingdom and patience which are in Jesus', RV. He was incarcerated in the isle called Patmos on account of the word of God and the testimony of Jesus, see vv. 2, 9. He was 'in the Spirit' (is the capital necessary, or is there an allusion to his own spirit?) on the Lord's day. This does not appear to relate to the day of the Lord; we suggest it does not refer to the first day of the week, but is the counterpart of man's day, 1 Cor. 4. 3 RV marg. Here in this book we have the Lord's judgement, estimate and account of things – how He looks at and regards them. Things are shown in their true hue in this book.

John sees the Lord Jesus in the role of an Inspector Judge walking in the midst of the seven golden lampstands which are the seven churches. The title 'Son of man', whenever used of Him prophetically, has to do with judgement and in this role He is here seen. He is clearly to be identified with the man in Daniel 10. 5, each of course being the Lord Jesus Christ. His breasts – His affections – are governed by divine principles. His love is not reckless. He is 'the ancient of days' with white hair and long experience. Absolute purity marks Him (white) and His assessments. Nothing escapes His notice, His eyes are as a flame of fire. His feet are as if they had been burnished in a furnace, and had they not? Was ever furnace hotter than that into which He went? Thus in His experience of the heat of divine judgement against sin, He must so act wherever He finds it. His word is as irresistible as many waters. In His right hand, under His control, are seven stars, and out of His mouth goes a two-edged sword, sharp, just and well-balanced. His countenance was as the sun shining in His strength, reminiscent of the day of transfiguration on the mount, Matt. 17. 2.

Who is surprised that John fell at His feet as dead? But how wonderful are the re-assuring words that identified the One of the vision as the Man of Calvary, the Christ of glory, He who was from everlasting to everlasting, the first and the last, the eternal One, He who became dead voluntarily (note R.V. marg. 'became') and who now lives again eternally triumphant over death and Hades! Whatever appearances now may be, however they may seem to contradict our wishes, here is One who is beyond all the limits of time, come into time, wrought gloriously on earth, and now stands supreme over heaven, earth, and hell.

In this manner the Apocalypse is introduced to us.

Things Which Are

INTRODUCTION

REVELATION 2-3

THERE ARE THREE WAYS in which these letters, recorded in Revelation 2 and 3, may be considered: (1) as written to seven actual churches existing in John's day and representative of the general condition of that day; (2) as having a message for God's people throughout the whole Christian era, no matter where they are found; and (3) as delineating the successive stages in the history of Christendom from apostolic times to our present day.

Some dissent as to (3) because the churches of John's time could never have understood the letters in that way and, indeed, were not intended to do so. But the remarkable agreement between this foreshadowing and the later history is too plain to be ignored. Moreover, such a foreshadowing in scripture is not new. Did the children of Israel understand the prophetic meaning of their sundry feasts recorded in Leviticus 23? Were they intended to do so? Yet looking back from our present day we can now understand their typical and prophetic significance. In this series we shall make reference to points in the letters which coincide with the later history. Plainly John's contemporaries knew nothing of this later history, but the passage of time sheds light on God's word everywhere.

If, as we believe, chapters 2 and 3 recorded the 'things which are', Rev. 1. 19, it is reasonable to regard them as setting out the present age from its inception to its consummation – the whole era in all its facets. Much is lost if the interpretation of these letters is limited to the conditions of the times in which they were written. The conditions recorded in the seven letters may be traced throughout the two millenniums since Pentecost. Similarly, the general decline from pristine brightness to Christless profession may be traced historically throughout the age.

The seven letters have a general similar pattern. Each is written to the 'angel' of the church. Although the word 'angel' may be rendered 'messenger', it is not clear how a messenger from Patmos to the respective cities could be blamed for existing conditions. And it is the 'angel' who is blamed. These 'angels' are symbolized by 'seven stars' and stars are guides; for example, the 'star in the east' led to the Saviour. Jude, conversely, speaks of 'wandering stars'. As the local church is symbolized by a lampstand denoting a plurality of persons, so we suggest that the 'stars' symbolize the 'angels' or a plurality of persons which constitute the responsible guiding element in the church. It would be contrary to the tenor of the New Testament to regard the 'angel' as the Minister or the Pastor. The scriptures recognize no such thing as one man entrusted with the care of a church; it is always a plurality who share that responsibility; see Acts 20. 28; Phil. 1. 1.

They are sent to 'the church in' such and such a place. This is so in every case (see the Revised Version). They were congregations of believers in the Lord Jesus Christ, administratively independent of each other. Not one is given the task of rectifying another; each is directly responsible to the Author of the letter. It is not one lampstand with a multiplicity of branches, but seven distinct lampstands (not candlesticks which are self-consuming, but *lampstands* dependent on exterior material to be the source of light) not federated together. They are golden *lampstands*, that is, they are a divine testimony set in the midst of surrounding darkness.

The manner in which the Lord is described at the beginning of each letter is specially suitable to the state concerned; this we shall see as we proceed. 'I know' occurs in each letter, the verb being cognate with 'I see'. In all but two there are complaints, the exceptions being the letters to Smyrna and Philadelphia. In each there is a promise to the 'overcomer'.

The overcomer does not denote a specially pious kind of Christian but every genuine believer. It is a question of what is

44

genuine. It is a mistake to suppose that everyone associated with the early or modern churches is real. The genuineness of one's profession is proved by his continuance; see Col. 1. 23; Heb. 3. 6. A believer may, like Gad, be overcome, but he overcomes at last. It is not the reverses but the final victory that counts. Only two classes are found in Revelation 21. 7-8; all are in one class or the other.

The promises remind us of Old Testament history: the first takes us back to Eden; the second to the affliction in Egypt; the third to the wilderness and its manna; the fourth to the victories of Joshua; the fifth to the days of the Babylonish captivity and the preserved Israelite registers; the sixth to the time of the restored remnant and the rebuilding of the temple under Ezra; and lastly the seventh to the days of Malachi and its lukewarmness; see Mal. 1. 10; 3. 14.

The word of Christ to the angel is the voice of the Spirit to the churches: what He says to one He says to all. It is 'he that hath an ear' and 'to him that overcometh'. We must on no account miss their present lessons in a pre-occupation with their historic or prophetic character.

Historically these letters denote seven moral conditions then existing and found at any time during the present age. Ephesus was a loveless church; Smyrna a persecuted one; Pergamos a worldly one; Thyatira a corrupt church; Sardis a reformed church; Philadelphia an evangelistic church and Laodicea a lukewarm church. We should inquire, what is the kind of church in which I am?

Prophetically these letters set forth the main features of the history of Christendom. Ephesus relates to apostolic times; Smyrna to the subsequent period of severe persecution; Pergamos-relates to the times of Constantine when the church was united with the state; Thyatira to the dark middle ages; Sardis speaks of the times of reformation when there was a failure to return to the fountain head of Holy Scripture; Philadelphia to the evangelistic period which followed; Laodicea, it is submitted, plainly depicts our own times when, as to Christendom, Christ is outside.

We have spoken of Christendom, which is to be distinguished from the church. The former relates to the sphere of Christian profession in which there are real and false; genuine and spurious. The true church embraces only those who are genuine. These letters envisage the presence of others who are far from what followers of Christ should be. As with the kingdom of the heavens, there are here wheat and chaff, wheat and tares, good fish and bad, treasure and leaven, pearl and bird-harbouring tree, wise and foolish virgins, faithful and wicked servants, sheep and goats. It is the sphere of religious profession and the Lord is seen walking in its midst, perceiving everything, judging all, rebuking, warning, promising.

Principles which should govern local church order and purity are not found here. Paul deals with these things in the Corinthian letters and the Pastoral Epistles. One cannot be excommunicated from Christendom, though one may be from a local church. On the other hand, every professor (true and false) is inescapably in Christendom.

Laodicea is warned that, unless it repents, the Lord is about to spew it out of His mouth. When the rapture takes place the empty Christless form will have been spewed out, those who are the 'overcomers', the genuine believers, having been removed to heaven. It is instructive to note that the church is nowhere seen again in the book of Revelation until the latter part of chapter 19.

EPHESUS

REVELATION 2. 1-7

THE BEGINNING of the Christian work of God in this city is recounted in Acts 18. 19 to 19. 20. There are many additional allusions to it in Paul's letter to the Ephesian church which will well repay searching out. The believers began with a zealous love for Christ which caused them to burn their books instead of selling them. Had they sold them, they would have spread the poison and retained the proceeds. But they suffered the loss. A little later their love was still aflame and Paul experienced this on calling the elders to him at Miletus, Acts 20. 17-38. Some years later their love was still aglow, and Paul was able to feed them with strong meat contained in his prison Epistle Ephesians, but he could not do this at Corinth, 1 Cor. 3. 2. Years rolled by, and some thirty years later they had left their first love, a departure that would result in Christ being ultimately outside the door, Rev. 3. 20. Whether this first love should be interpreted as a person or as a thing little matters. One should read Jeremiah 2. 2ff. in this connection; it is most revealing as to how the Lord reacts to such ungrateful requital.

This decline took place despite the fact that there were works, labour, patience, and even intolerance of evil persons and false apostles. There was unabating labour for His name's sake. Actively they wrought; passively they endured. But the motive spring of love was lacking. Ponder the Lord's interrogation of Peter, 'Lovest thou me?', John 21. 15-17, and the affirmation of Paul, 'the love of Christ constraineth us', 2 Cor. 5. 14. How easy it is to engage in a multiplicity of church activities, yet for all to be done by promptings unworthy of Christ. What a contrast is this with the motivation of the Thessalonians' service, namely their 'work of faith, and labour of love, and patience of hope', 1 Thess. 1. 3.

What Paul had foreseen when addressing the elders at Miletus had now taken place, Acts 20. 29. 'Evil men' and 'false apostles' had attempted to come in, but the church could not bear the former, and had by trial discovered the spuriousness of the latter since they lacked the requisite credentials. These 'false apostles', 2 Cor. 11. 5; 12. 11, had previously beguiled the Corinthians, but they had not so far caught the Ephesians. The 'elect lady' was warned by John against such persons, 2 John 9.

The pronouns 'thou' and 'thy', which so frequently recur, refer to the 'angel', who is symbolized by the 'star' denoting, as we have said, the responsible guiding element in the local church. It is this overseership which is first praised for what is praiseworthy and then is held responsible for the failure in the church. Overseers nowadays should mark this well.

To their credit stands their hatred of the deeds of the Nicolaitans, a hatred shared by the Lord. There has been much conjecture about these Nicolaitans. It does not appear to be tenable to associate them with Nicolas of Acts 6; the presumed evidence is far too flimsy. Nor does history know of any such sect in these early times. The etymology of the word must be examined for any symbolic meaning. The word Nicolaitans is comprised of two Greek words: *nico*, to conquer; and *laos*, people. It therefore suggests a caste which dominated the common people in the church, much like those who would lord a heritage, 1 Pet. 5. 3. Diotrephes at Ephesus (presumably), whose self-assertive, dictatorial and exclusive behaviour involved even the apostle John, 3 John 9-10, is a typical case.

If this be the true explanation, it is not to be wondered at that clerical commentators do not mention it, for their very position would be condemned thereby. Happily, many of them are far better than the position which they hold; some indeed have had the courage to abandon it. But nothing scriptural whatever can be said in support of any form of clerisy; it is contrary to all New Testament teaching.

The Ephesians had *left their first love*. They should therefore remember from whence they had fallen and repent and return to their original position. Adam fell from his exalted position due to his not loving the Lord with all his heart. The record of Rebekah in Genesis 27 contrasts unfavourably with that of chapter 24. Adam lost his place in the garden and if Ephesus would not repent they, too, would lose their place. The lampstand would be removed, and this, in fact, actually took place. We should point out that not every local church that has ceased to exist has been thus removed by the Lord; there may be many other contributing causes. But North Africa stands as a solemn witness; once many lampstands were there, but behold it now! The Lord who ever walks in judicial garb in their midst removes this and that lampstand from the place of testimony because true motive is lacking. The area is thereby left in utter darkness.

The overcomer is promised precisely what our first parents forfeited. He would eat of the tree of life which is in the midst of the paradise of God. Adam and Eve were removed from the earthly garden, but God's paradise is now in heaven, 2 Cor. 12. 4.

The phrase 'tree of life' is remarkable, for the Greek word for 'tree' denotes not a *living tree* but a *dead tree stump*. On such the Lord was hanged, but as a result of His death we live. Ponder Revelation 22 verses 2, 14 and 19 RV. These verses have to do with those who are admitted to, and those who are barred from, the tree of life.

The clarion call of this letter is to *remember*, to *repent* and to *repeat*. *Remember* demands a looking back to the former condition; *repent* entails a consideration of the present state; and *repeat* envisages a recovery for the future. This recovery can only be achieved by the removal of every other rival claimant to our love, and to make Christ Himself our 'first love'. All else will then be given its proper relative place. Overseers need to learn afresh that they are firmly held in His right hand, and are responsible to Him for those whom He has entrusted to their care. Saints need to learn afresh that the Lord is walking in the midst of the lampstands and from Him nothing can be concealed. An awareness of His presence and a sight of His Majesty as detailed in chapter 1 would evoke the awe and love of His people. Have we lost that awareness?

SMYRNA

REVELATION 2. 8-11

PERSECUTION HAS characterized the history of the church from its very beginning. Peter, John and Stephen were its early victims, and the saints, Acts 8. 1, as well as Paul and his companions, were later included. But there was worse to come and the Smyrnean believers are enjoined not to fear 'the things thou art about to suffer', Rev. 2. 10 RV The devil was 'about to cast some' of them into prison in order that the whole church might be tested, 2. 10 RV. When 'some' suffer, the whole company is affected.

They are called upon to be 'faithful unto death' and such are promised a victor's 'crown of life'. Who, indeed, was better fitted to write in such terms than the Lord Himself? Although He is the 'first and the last', although He is God, yet when He became Man, He 'died and lived again', and this was due, among other things, to His faithfulness. Should they suffer even unto death, they would then be but following in His train.

Because of their faith, they had suffered from those who claimed to be the people of God, namely from those who said they were Jews but really were not, 'For he is not a Jew, which is one outwardly', Rom. 2. 28. To be one of God's real people the heart must be right. Yet has it not been a feature of the whole of the so-called Christian era that saints have been persecuted by those who have adhered to a Judaistic form of Christianity with its priests, vestments, altar, incense and ritual? Even in the earliest days of Christianity it was the Jewish religionist who persecuted the disciples, and as time went on, that which developed into the Roman Catholic church became the arch-inquisitor against the true people of God. They could say nothing too bad against them (blasphemy) nor do anything too cruel (tribulation).

The well-known persecutions such as that under Diocletian, following the early days of the church's pilgrimage, were designed to test the saints. Ten days were proposed to test Rebekah's decision, Gen. 24. 55; Nehemiah, Neh. 4. 12, and Daniel and his friends, Dan. 1. 12, were all likewise tested for a similar period.

It would seem from the omission of the mention of 'works' in this letter (see Rev. 2. 9 RV) that the saints at Smyrna were so bitterly persecuted that activity in the service of God was rendered almost impossible. They were between the upper and nether millstones, so great was their 'tribulation'. They had doubtless suffered the 'spoiling of their goods', so great was their material 'poverty'. But actually they were rich for 'all things are yours . . . and ye are Christ's; and Christ is God's', 1 Cor. 3. 21-23; spiritual riches cannot be confiscated.

Virtually a conflict was raging between the powers of light and darkness; on the one side was ranged the Lord of glory and His people, and on the other Satan, that is 'the devil', and his dupes. He is ever an imitator. The true bride of Christ is counterfeited by the whore; the true apostles by the false apostles; the true church by the 'synagogue of Satan'. This is not Protestantism versus Romanism, but true believers versus false religionists, no matter by what name they may be called. As when the Lord was here, so now the powers of darkness sought to extinguish the true light, but despite the appearance of glory, 'the darkness overcame it not', John 1. 5 RV marg. The true light still shone, and those who loved not their lives to death would receive the victor's crown of life in resurrection and glory, as did their Lord, Heb. 2. 9.

Two things were required of them: (1) *fearlessness* and (2) *faithfulness*. How often did the Lord call for these things in the days of His flesh! See Luke 12. 4, 7, 32; Matt. 24. 45; 25. 23. And how greatly did these things shine in His earthly course! For the sufferings of Gethsemane did not spring from fear of death but rather from fear of God, and the opposition of His enemies was because of His faithfulness to His God.

The *overcomer* is assured immunity from the 'second death'. This 'second death' is that which follows upon death and Hades being cast into the lake of fire. Ponder carefully Revelation 20. 5, 11-15, wherein are defined those who will be exempt from, and those who will experience this 'second death'. It is such a death as will entail the re-union of body with soul, indestructibly to be conscious of the punitive wrath of God upon them.

It follows that, since no genuine believer will ever be lost, then every such believer must be an overcomer. John 5. 24 is crystal clear on this point. No interpretation of any of these promises to the 'overcomer' must be allowed to upset that statement. But we should search our hearts to assure ourselves before God, and, having confidence toward God, we may rejoice in the assurance that, whatever injustice we have suffered in this life because of our faith, we shall be done no injustice by falling to the second death. The negative 'shall not be hurt of the second death' in verse 11 is very emphatic.

This short letter read as relating to the circumstances of their immediate days shows how real is the Lord's sympathy with those who were then treading a path similar to that which He had trodden. Its preservation to our times is designed to encourage all saints of every era that death does not end all; it is to be followed by a life that cannot be touched. 'Weeping may endure for a night, but joy cometh in the morning', Ps. 30. 5. When read prophetically, the letter shows how true it is to facts as they developed, the bitter persecutions of the second and third centuries of the Christian age being witness.

How nobly Christians acted when facing death may be learned by reading of the persecutions not only of Diocletian and other remote times, but of Philip II of Spain and Mary Queen of Scots, and many another abuser of secular power who broke themselves on the anvil of God.

PERGAMOS

REVELATION 2. 12-17

AS WE HAVE ALREADY SEEN, the Lord presents Himself to each church in a manner appropriate to its condition and His intention of action. Hence here He has the 'sharp sword with two edges' with which He will come and fight against those who hold the doctrine of Balaam and of the Nicolaitans. The sword of His word, Eph. 6. 17, will test their 'doctrine' and judge it.

What were *deeds* at Ephesus, Rev. 2. 6, have now become an established *doctrine* at Pergamos, 2. 15. The principle was not merely existent, it was held as a doctrinal tenet. The simple scriptural method of church government by elders (otherwise called overseers, Acts 20. 28) was displaced, and a recognized caste of persons with grades of authority from the highest to the lowest was now substituted.

This was brought into being when Constantine terminated the persecutions and patronized the church. The union of religion with the state was, in principle, as old as the days of Balaam, when the false prophet, in order to gain the king's honours and rewards, worked under the direction of Balak the king of Moab, both of them being bent on cursing the people of God, Numbers chs. 22-24. A similar alliance is seen in the case of Ahab (the political power) and the dark sinister Jezebel, both of whom were criminally guilty of both the murder of Naboth and the confiscation of his property, 1 Kings 21. So it was with Herod, Herodias, and her daughter; all three were responsible for the beheading of John Baptist, Mark 6. 17-29. So, too, the chief priests and elders, aided and abetted by a great multitude, arrested the Lord in the garden of Gethsemane. The book of the Acts commences with Jerusalem the religious centre and ends with Rome the political centre; both of these cities persecuted the early Christians. The principle is the same today with Rome who claims both imperial and religious powers. And in a breakaway section therefrom there exists the union of the church with the state. Men sell their so-called spiritual services for stipends and honours bestowed by the secular power.

The seed was found at Ephesus, but the developed plant at Pergamos. This place is called 'where Satan's throne is', Rev. 2. 13 RV. It is said to have been the first city in Asia with a temple for the worship of Augustus (Octavius Caesar), so that political and religious power were centred in one person. The Lord recognized the difficulty of the situation, the church being located in such a hot-bed of serpent worship – 'where Satan dwelleth', 2. 13. It was specially commendable, therefore, that they had held fast His name, and had not denied His faith even in the days when a faithful witness named Antipas had forfeited his life for Christ's sake. They were not ashamed of the name 'Christian' nor had they apostatized from the faith. It would have been all too easy to have done so, as the Epistle to the Hebrews shows.

But against them was the fact that they had in their midst those who had flouted the decree sent forth from Jerusalem forbidding fornication and eating things sacrificed to idols, Acts 15. 23-29. Whatever Paul wrote to the Corinthians touching this matter was not a repudiation of the earlier decree, but rather a direction to the saints that they should not make needless enquiries as to the history of the food which they had purchased or which was put before them in the house of an unbeliever. The use to which the food had previously been put did not affect adversely the food itself. But if it came to light that it had been offered to idols the situation was different; it must not then be eaten. Thus the apostles at Jerusalem, Paul in writing to Corinth, and John here in the apocalyptic letters are in full agreement with each other.

Balaam's evil counsel after his enforced inability to utter curses against God's people, Num. 25, is here referred to. The doctrine which was both morally and religiously corrupt was condemned. Its counterpart today is the new morality which sets aside God's institution of marriage, Heb. 13. 4. It cannot be infringed with impunity; whoremongers and adulterers God will judge, though human authorities fail to do so.

This kind of thing should never have gained a footing in the Pergamos church. It called for quick action and suppression, Rev. 2. 16. Balaam could not turn God away from Israel so he sought to turn Israel away from God. In like manner the persecution of Smyrna had not extinguished the light of testimony but had purified its shining. Satan would, therefore, adopt more cunning methods to put out the lamp.

Teaching and practice are joined together. Each is adversely or favourably affected by the other. If the teaching is corrupt the morals will be corrupted also. Whether in the spiritual or physical sphere, fornication is the antithesis of that which is demanded by espousal.

The doctrine of the Nicolaitans is brought in here as a further aggravation of their faults. The evil seems to be almost identical, though viewed from slightly different angles, with that of Balaam. The etymology of the Hebrew word Balaam appears to be either that of *lording or devouring the people*, while that of Nicolaitan is *conquering the people*. We repeat that doubtless there are persons who hold ecclesiastical office in both Established and Nonconformist circles whose hearts are far removed from either of these two evils; they neither wish to dominate nor to fleece the people in their care. Yet the fact is that the very principle of their office has within it the germs of these two things, which in their fully developed state enslave their dupes.

HATCH in his *Bampton Lecture* writes: 'The fourth century is important in the history of Christian organization as being the period in which church officers lost their primitive character and became a separate class'. He adds, 'For this change there were two chief causes, (1) the recognition of Christianity by the state and (2) the influence of monasticism'.

The Lord warns of speedy action should they not repent; He will fight against them with the sword of His mouth. That He waits so long displays His longsuffering patience, but Revelation 17. 14 shows that He will implement His warning.

The overcomer is promised the hidden manna in contrast with the things sacrificed to idols. The provision for God's redeemed people in the wilderness, and which was put into the ark, is to become the specially enjoyed portion of those who refuse the blandishments of Balak. The manna contained in the golden pot, Heb. 9. 4, hidden from the eyes of men, speaks of Christ, the bread of life come down from heaven as the source of sustenance for His pilgrim people. The 'white stone' or pebble was used for very many purposes and therefore to limit it to one thing would be unduly to restrict its significance. It might speak of acquittal, or special privilege, or an indication of the estimate by the donor of the person whose name appears on the stone. The recipient will have a special and private awareness of the character that he has formed and which has gained his Lord's approval. He will know what the Lord thinks of him, whatever may be the thoughts of others.

THYATIRA

REVELATION 2. 18-29

IT IS LITTLE WONDER that when the world patronizes the church, the state of the professing system becomes worse. Whenever there is departure from the simple ways that be in Christ, there is bound to be an ever speedy decline into abysmal corruption. So it was in this church.

We do not forget that these letters represent states that existed concurrently when they were first addressed to the churches. Nor do we forget that the seven conditions are to be found at any time on earth. But the remarkable progressive corruption which set in consequent upon Constantine having patronized and adopted Christianity (though he himself was not baptized till near the end of his life) is clearly set out in the letter now before us.

Lydia, a seller of purple, belonged to Thyatira, Acts 16. 14-15. It was a place noted for its contributions to the glamour of this world, and that atmosphere had crept into the professing church. But there was One walking in the midst of the lampstands named the Son of God whose feet were like unto burnished brass, and whose eyes were 'like unto a flame of fire', Rev. 2. 18. Nothing escaped His notice; His eyes detect everything, try everything, and He consumes all that is evil. He searches the reins and the hearts. He will most surely come and judge. He who had Himself trodden the paths of judgement, whose own feet had been burned as in a furnace, could do none other than judge sin wherever He found it. Being the Son of God He possesses every divine attribute. He knows all, is everywhere, and can do everything. With such an One the Thyatiran church had to do. And so do we all.

There was much to their credit: works, love, service, faith, patience; indeed there was more activity than hitherto, 'the last works are more than the first', 2. 19 RV. But there was cause for stern censure. If in the case of Pergamos there was evil within (Nicolaitanism) and evil without (Balaamism), here matters were worse. It was a woman that was inside, tolerated, and out of her proper sphere. Although Paul had written 'I suffer not a woman to teach, nor to usurp authority over the man', 1 Tim. 2. 12, Jezebel was suffered to teach, and in so doing to seduce the Lord's servants into religious and moral corruption, flouting the apostolic decree of Acts 15. Of course, the reference is not to the historic Jezebel, but to her then, modern counterpart. She may, at the time of writing, have been an actual person but she stands for a tolerated corrupt principle. She called herself a prophetess, claiming the right to speak for God, but unlike Anna and Philip's four daughters she was a false prophetess. The Old Testament history of Jezebel is full of instruction. She was the wicked power behind the apostate throne of Ahab. She had no scruples and cared nothing whatsoever for the divine Decalogue. What did it matter to her if she bowed down to idols? or if she falsely accused? or murdered? or what did she care if she stole Naboth's vineyard? She may paint her face but it did not improve her heart. The doom of her counterpart is certain, foreshadowed by God, and will, as was the case of the original woman, be implemented by men. She 'sat as queen'; she rode the beast; but she will be turned off, cast down, and burned with fire. Her end will be bitter indeed, Rev. 17. 16.

No doubt something of this in principle happened in the days immediately consequent upon Luther's protests. The power of Rome and her children suffered much when she was cast into a bed of sickness, and into great tribulation. History has a way of repeating itself because the same causes produce the same effects. And each recurrence seems to grow more intense so that the 'great tribulation' here alluded to will ultimately be experienced by apostate Christendom on a more severe scale, 2. 22. The reader should study the history of Jezebel's daughter Athaliah, and grandson Ahaziah; it is prophetic of what is yet to be enacted on a far wider plane.

This 'great tribulation' is to be distinguished from 'the tribulation, the great one' yet to be and which will have Israel for its centre, though the whole world will be involved in its effects, 7. 14. But in each case, both the religious system and that which is in any way immorally associated with it will be involved in the conflagration.

God is longsuffering, for judgement is His strange work. He has no delight in it, however inevitable His righteousness may make it. 'I gave her space to repent of her fornication', 2. 21. Spiritual fornication is the *illicit* alliance of the church with the world.

The true church having been espoused to Christ does not give her affections to the world, but that Christendom has done. The nominal church and the world are inseparably united so that to distinguish one from the other is no easy matter.

The warning could not be more plain; sickness, tribulation and death, in which her posterity (her children) would be involved as well as herself, would surely come upon them. It would be a lesson to all observers – all the churches will know that the Lord whose eyes are as a flame of fire 'searcheth the reins and hearts' – both motives and thoughts will be discovered and exposed, 2. 23. She did not will to repent, v. 21 RV, of her fornication. She had no sense of shame nor of her disloyalty to Christ. Therefore judgement was inevitable, a judgement which would be proportionate to personal and individual guilt, 'everyone of you according to your works', 2. 23.

The longsuffering of God explains the mysterious continuance of persecution of the truly godly by the religious world; see Luke 18.

1-7. The long history of the dark middle ages, when Christendom was in the depths of corruption, is a story often told. The sufferings of the Lord's real people at the hands of the nominal professors are an irremovable stain on so-called church history.

Yet there were a faithful few in Thyatira who did not hold this teaching and did not know 'the depths of Satan' as it is called, 2. 24. Their hearts and interests lay in 'the deep things of God', 1 Cor. 2. 10. The evil schemes and thoughts of Satan were foreign to them.

Though 'the rest in Thyatira' were but a small remnant, yet those all searching eyes had not failed to notice them, Rev. 2. 24. He knew how hard pressed they were and that they could scarce bear any further burden. They had not been ensnared by Satan's imitative wiles, but how long would this last? The Lord would not allow their burden to be further increased, but enjoined them to 'hold fast' what they had till He should come, 2. 25. They were persecuted by Jezebel and her kind, as were the Lord's prophets and Naboth of old, 1 Kings 18. 13; ch. 21. They were victims of men like Diotrephes, Hymenaeus and Philetus, and Jannes and

Jambres. The godly poor and faithful believers were hounded to death by men bearing pompous ecclesiastical titles and wearing deceptive robes. The reader should peruse E. H. BROADBENT's book *The Pilgrim Church* or other like works to enlighten himself of the co-existence of apostate Christendom with the true godly Christian. He will then see the benefit of reading this correspondence not only in the light of the times when it was first written, and not only in the light of times later than these which have now passed into history, but in the light of our present times. Signs are not wanting nowadays that the organized World Council of Churches is hostile to the truly faithful.

That mistakes were made in the middle ages, when the faithful took the sword and besmirched their record with atrocities, is all too true. The Lord does not want that kind of thing. Forcibly pulling up the tares will damage the wheat. He requires 'the rest' (that is, the small remnant) to be relentless in holding on to their possessions. They were given the hope of His coming; 'till I come'. For 'he that overcometh, and keepeth my works unto the end' shall be saved, 2. 26. A firm refusal to jettison the faith once for all delivered to the saints, a stubborn refusal to give it up, is what He requires of His faithful few. His coming will relieve the pressure, justify the course taken and put an end to their persecution.

The overcomer is promised that he will be given authority over the nations. This is the very thing that apostate Christendom had claimed, still claims though under restraint now, and will yet claim and obtain in days before the end. But the One to whom all authority in heaven and earth has been given promises that that authority shall be wrenched from them and He will take it and share it with His own (compare Ps. 2. 9; Ps. 110; Rev. 19. 15; these passages shed mutual light on each other).

The *'morning star'* shines in the darkness before the dawn of day. This is the peculiar portion of the church to enjoy, 2 Pet. 1. 19; Rev. 22. 16. It will be at the dawn of day that we shall come forth with Him 'to reign over the earth'. But we shall have first gone to the Father's house, John 14. 3, in order to come forth in regal array. This is our 'morning star' hope. This star shines in the darkness, in the heavens, from whence we expect a Saviour who will take us away before the world's darkest hour.

The word 'rule', Rev. 2. 27, is actually 'shepherd', for the Lord will, when He reigns, have both a shepherd heart and an iron rod. History records the lamentable failure of man in this union of two apparently opposite roles, for either the ruler has been despotic without mercy or merciful and thereby degenerating into weakness. The two principles will be happily blended in the Perfect Ruler of men.

In view of all this, let us 'hold fast the traditions, even as they were delivered to us', 1 Cor. 11. 2 RV. Let us 'hold the traditions' which we have been taught whether by word or by apostolic epistles, 2 Thess. 2. 15, the tradition of 'the faith which was once for all delivered unto the saints', Jude 3 RV.

SARDIS

REVELATION 3. 1-6

THE CHIEF THING that marked this church was a lifeless profession, a denial of what was professed. The church had a name to live, but it was actually dead. Its reputation belied its state. Its character was cold, bleak, dead, mere formal orthodoxy. Reality can only be produced by the Spirit of God working in the church without hindrance. And this will be effected when the guides in a local church function according to the mind of God. No wonder, then, the Lord is here shown as 'he that hath the seven Spirits of God, and the seven stars', 3. 1. For the Spirit was sent by the Father and the Son, and scriptural guides are appointed by Him, Acts 20. 28. But while the name of Christ is attached to Christendom, it is dead; there are many churches in all branches of Christendom, Protestant as well as Romanist, utterly devoid of life.

Protestantism was brought into existence in consequence of the abuses of popery, but in such a revolt there was not a full return to the simplicity of holy scripture. The Lord had not found these works perfect – they had not returned all the way, Rev. 3. 2. They should, therefore, remember how they had received and first heard; that word they should keep, and repent of their failure, 3. 3. The scriptures are the sole valid authority; to it the protesters of Luther's day and later returned in part; they began reformation but did not complete it.

This was doubtless the state of the Sardian church at that time. There was reform but they had not gone back to the fountain of truth and made adjustments in accordance with it. They had made a beginning but did not finish. It has been so throughout the Christian era. It certainly was so at the time of the Reformation when there was a revolt against popery but things were retained and others were introduced which did not accord with holy scripture. John exhorted the believers to 'hold fast that which they had heard from the beginning' of Christianity, 1 John 2. 24. Paul also enjoined Timothy to 'hold fast the form of sound words' which he had heard from him, 2 Tim. 1. 13. The Lord has always had the few who have made scripture their sole guide for faith and conduct. Most have done otherwise: they have retained whatever was pleasing to the senses; they have kept the name but in revolting against a corrupt form they have created a dead form of religious activities.

It is the responsibility of overseers to 'strengthen the things which remain, that are ready to die'. As an army commander would rally his men after a defeat and re-equip and encourage them, so elders should rally and hearten the saints. How can this be done? By returning to the scriptures; plausibility, expediency, conformity are no safe guides. The overseers must be 'watchful'; they must keep awake and do as Peter was enjoined, 'strengthen thy brethren', Luke 22. 32.

The Lord warns that should there be failure in watching He would come at an altogether unknown hour and 'as a thief'. Now the Lord does not so come for the church. There is not the slightest hint of a thief-like coming in John 14. 3; 1 Thess. 4. 13ff.; 1 Cor. 15. 50ff. But the words are used in the case of the day of the Lord when He will introduce His judgements on men; see 1 Thess. 5. 2; Matt. 24. 43. Christendom, it must be borne in mind, continues to the time when the beast casts off the woman, for the woman and Christendom are identical but the church, the bride of Christ, is taken away some time before that occurs. The rapture will be the fulfilment of the promise to Philadelphia in Revelation 3. 10; this will also be the time of the spewing out of the Lord's mouth of the professing thing spoken of in the Laodicean letter.

As in Thyatira, there are in Sardis *a few who 'have not defiled their garments'* with the corruption of lifeless Christendom. These are promised that they will 'walk with' the Lord in white. What a privilege to walk with the Lord; could there be a greater honour? 'In white' speaks of the character that these saints have wrought out on earth; this will then become manifest in open display with the Lord in glory; see 19. 8 RV.

Someone has said that majorities should be tolerant, and minorities should be courageous. God is not on the side of the big battalions; He seems to delight in the 'few'. How many were saved in Noah's day? 'A few, that is eight'. Are there few that shall be saved? Apparently, if Sardis is a guide.

To the overcomer there is a threefold promise: (1) he shall be arrayed in white garments. He will then be seen to be in the right, however much he may have been maligned before. (2) 'I will not blot out his name out of the book of life'. Although they may have been regarded as criminals or heretics or worse by men and, in consequence, had their name expunged either from the citizens' or church registers, they may rest assured that their names will not be expunged from the book of life. We cannot stress too strongly that every genuine believer is an overcomer, and of such none will ever perish, John 10. 28. But genuineness is proved by continuity. A Peter may deny his Lord in a moment of unguardedness, but this was not apostasy; he was restored, (3) 'I will confess his name before my

Father, and before his angels'. Believers will be acknowledged by Him, whilst all other men will be disowned.

No doubt these overcomers are among the twenty-four elders who are clothed in white and crowned with victor's crowns referred to in Revelation 4. 4. They will then be in the enjoyment of the fulfilment of this very emphatic promise, 'I will never, never, blot out his name'.

The prime lesson of this letter is to warn all against a carnal security. Read the Lord's own words in Matthew 10. 32-33. If the Lord denies anyone in that day it is tantamount to blotting out his name from the book of life. A religious form, having been maintained but lacking vitality and reality, will avail nothing then.

PHILADELPHIA

REVELATION 3. 7-13

TO THIS CHURCH the Lord presents Himself as irresistibly Sovereign. He is 'true' to all that His name in every aspect implies and he has the royal key of David; He possesses sovereign rights on earth as well as in heaven. He, therefore, can open and none can shut, and *vice versa*, 3. 7.

What is the 'door opened' which He has given to this church? Several conjectures have been made, but by a consideration of such passages as Acts 14. 27; 1 Cor. 16. 9; 2 Cor. 2. 12; Col. 4. 3, it would seem that it is a door of opportunity to proclaim the word. Paul had himself taken advantage of the opened door and had proclaimed faith among the Gentiles; such an opportunity on a large scale had occurred at Ephesus; a door had been opened at Troas.

If we regard these letters as depicting the outline of the history of Christendom, it would seem to denote the evangelistic era which has embraced our own times as well as earlier. But while such doors were opened in apostolic times, and while they have been opened here and there throughout the whole Christian era, there has been, as history attests, a special period of unique evangelistic opportunity. It may be that the day of Gentile opportunity is closing and the Lord Himself is shutting the doors now. Time will tell, for we may be assured that, whatever men and governments may determine, until the Lord shuts the door no other person can do so. We must use to the full our present privileges; they may not last long.

It appears to be too general to say that this is the key of entrance into the kingdom, since that has been existent right from the days when Peter opened it to the Jew on the day of Pentecost and to the Gentiles in the house of Cornelius. Much less does it relate to entrance into the local church. That should have been open to every sterling Christian from the very beginning. It seems to accord with the tenor of the rest of the New Testament that this is the door of evangelistic opportunity.

It has been opened by One who is both holy and true – descriptions that are not infrequently used of the Lord Jesus. He was 'that holy thing' born of the virgin Mary and as the Holy One He gave the unction to all believers – the Holy Spirit. The word used for 'true' here denotes not so much true to His word (and that He ever is) but true to all that He Himself is – He is true to the promise of His name as well as of His lips.

The Lord acknowledges that this church had a little strength, and that they had been faithful both to His word and name. Though but a relatively feeble few, they had returned to the fountain head of divine truth, the scriptures, and in loyalty to Him who loved them, v. 9, had sought to keep it. There were others who, claiming to be the people of God ('Jews, and are not'), opposed them but from time to time have been compelled to acknowledge where the truth was. The opposition of the Jews to the gospel in apostolic times is seen clearly throughout the book of the Acts. Later, others have claimed to be God's people on earth and have been equally hostile to the simple preaching of the pure gospel. We need not name them; such claimants will readily come to mind.

To this church the Lord gives the promise of exemption from the *hour of trial* that is to come upon the habitable earth to put earth-dwellers to the test. Note carefully they are to be kept from the *hour*, not merely from the *trial*, 3. 10. The time of this special trial is the latter half of Daniel's seventieth week, but before even that week itself commences the church will have been raptured to heaven; see Rev. 17. 14.

. The words of the promise should be carefully noted. It is not a promise of being kept safely through the trial but being kept *out of* the hour of that trial. Space forbids the setting out of the full evidence in support of this. We did so partially in our previous series of articles[2] relating to prophetic future events. The Revised Version reading is very clear and assuring. Patience has been exercised by the saints on earth, a patience which is called 'my patience' for the Lord Himself in heaven is patiently waiting the fulfilment of the expected promise, Heb. 10. 13. That patience will be rewarded. 'Behold, I come quickly' is the promise by which the deliverance from the coming trial will be effected. Rev. 3. 11. No date or sign is given, but the saints are enjoined to hold fast what they had, things which the Lord acknowledged to exist – their strength, faithfulness and witness – in order that they lose not their victor's crown in that day. In 2 Samuel 12. 26ff. is recorded an instructive incident in which David was likely to have lost his royal rights over a city.

Thus the saints are encouraged to endure, being given the hope of the near return of their Lord with its consequent deliverance from the unequalled time of tribulation that will come upon the habitable earth. At the same time, they are reminded that the judgement-seat lies ahead when crowns will be given as rewards for service here, a reward of which they must see that no one robs them, Rev. 3. 11. Verse 10 is incapable of a satisfactory exposition if the prophetic view of the letters is rejected. Attempts have been made to construe the verse as if it were a promise of preservation in the trial itself, but that is not the meaning that the words convey. They promise immunity from the very hour of the trial, and if *one* is not here in the

---

[2] Future Events, pages 7-33.

hour of the trial, neither can *one* be in the trial of that hour. All faithful translations are unanimous.

The possibility of the loss of one's crown is envisaged in 1 Corinthians 3. 15; 9. 27; Luke 19. 26. It is neither possible for a child of God to lose any blessing given him in sovereign grace, nor to lose his place in the kingdom, but he may lose his reward and his crown. We cannot be too careful in this regard.

The overcomer will be made a pillar in the temple of God, out from which he will go no more, though he may have been expelled by men on earth, Rev. 3. 12. He will bear the name both of God and of His city. He will also have Christ's new name. The pillar denotes responsibility in the future as James, Cephas, and John were pillars in the early church. Gal. 2. 9. The frequency of the words 'my God' implies that the Lord has once been here on earth as dependent Man, and appealed to His God in His direst hour of need, Matt. 27. 46. The inscription of the names indicates both to whom the bearer of the name belongs and his place of residence. In a word, the whole of the promise denotes the inseparable union of the overcomer with God and His Christ. It may not be apparent now, but it will be then. Revelation 19. 13, 16 throw light on the 'name' and chapter 21 describes the 'New Jerusalem'. As a man may wear a cap on which the name and town of his employer are inscribed, so then the overcomer will bear in himself such an identification mark.

LAODICEA

REVELATION 3. 14-22

THIS IS THE LAST of the letters to the seven churches. Many more churches existed than these seven in John's day, but the Spirit selected these seven as representing seven conditions which may be found at all times. But they are dealt with in the order of Ephesus first and Laodicea last, the others coming in true sequence between, because they indicate the seven stages of the history of Christendom. Laodicea is its last stage before being spewed out of the Lord's mouth. That spewing will be when the Lord raptures the true saints and leaves behind, abandoned, the false and merely nominal thing. There is no mention in this letter of there being one genuine person in the church at Laodicea.

The letter is directed to a self-righteous and self-satisfied church, for so the name Laodicea apparently means. To that church the general Epistle to the Ephesians had presumably also circulated, and to them also had been read a special letter by Paul who reminded them that 'Christ is all, and in all' and that in Him 'are hid all the treasures of wisdom and knowledge', Col. 2. 3; 3. 11; 4. 16. How far they had strayed from these truths this letter reveals.

The Lord is presented as 'the faithful and true witness', Rev. 3. 14. If He has to inflict wounds, they are those of a friend. As a competent physician He will diagnose their trouble; He will hide nothing. He will be candid and true. He is also presented as the 'beginning of the creation of God', not that He was Himself a created Being for by Him all things were made, but He is the Source, the Beginning, the Originator of God's creation. He is also 'the Amen', the verifier of all the promises of God.

A grave warning is given, that unless the malady is cured there will be nothing but utter ruin. They will be spewed out of His mouth, much as one who is thirsty rejects water that is only tepid, neither cold nor hot. For the malady at Laodicea was not simple, it was compound. There was *indecision, independence* and *ignorance*.

There was *indecision*, for there was not found with them the utter coldness of absolute indifference to all things Christian, nor the keen and zealous propagation of true Christianity; they were neither one nor the other, but there was the intermediate lifeless formal shell, 3. 15. Much of this is evident today.

Then there was *independence*. 'I am rich, and increased with goods, and have need of nothing' nor of anyone. To the true riches in Christ they were strangers, but material wealth was theirs and on it their heart was set, 3. 17.

There was also *ignorance*. For they knew not that they were 'wretched, and miserable, and poor, and blind, and naked', 3. 17. These words cannot be said of any true believer, however cold in heart he may have become. They are true only of a Christless, formal, so-called Christian church, inside which Christ has no place. It is the last stage of Christendom before its final rejection.

The end of the book of Judges gives the record of blind Samson. The end of the kingdom of Judah was blind Zedekiah. The end of Judaism was the blind man of John 9 reminding the Pharisees of their blindness. The end of Christendom is blind Laodicea.

The Lord offers some plain advice, 'I counsel thee to buy', 3. 18. Now this word 'buy' seems strange though it has been used in Isaiah 55. 1; it implies that one gives up something in exchange for something else. This is so here. The Laodiceans are called upon to give up their indecision, independence, and ignorance and to accept from the Lord something else. So 'buy of me' and abandon that indecision which kept them from Him. So 'buy of me' and abandon that independence that said, I have need of nothing or no one. Yes, 'buy of me' those things which are real wealth, which they lacked; by so doing they would abandon their ignorance and acknowledge their true poverty-stricken condition. We repeat that it seems utterly impossible to apply these words to real believers however cold in heart they may have become. But they are applicable to false religionists, who are without Christ. They need the refined gold of the divine nature; they need the white raiment of divine righteousness; they need the eye salve of the Holy Spirit who will give inward sight, 3. 18. The cost involved is reasonable, logical, and inevitable, for until the counsel is accepted and acted on, the condition cannot be put right, but let the church show a readiness to acknowledge its utter badness and that its only hope is in Christ, then things can be adjusted.

The Lord then makes a pathetic appeal in 3. 20, a verse which has furnished many a preacher with a message to sinners. Go on, my brother, preach it yet again; it is most applicable. But never forget it really speaks of Christ outside the professing church, for long having knocked and still knocking at the door of this church, He expects a response, not from all but only from the individual. This shows how things have declined. This decline began with 'some' in the church, the church being as a whole fairly sound, 2. 15 RV. Then there was a remnant in the midst of a corrupt church, 'the rest', 2. 24. Then there were but a 'few names' in Sardis, 3. 4, that had not defiled their garments. Here Christ is altogether outside and He appeals for a response from someone. When He comes will He find faith on the earth?

We do not find here the logical working out of doctrinal arguments but the heartfelt utterances of One who is grieved. 'As many as I love, I rebuke and chasten; be zealous therefore and repent', 3. 19. This He says from outside, thus assuring any inside that they may count on His love and His faithfulness. For true love never glosses over sin, no more than a competent physician blinds himself to the grievous malady of his patient and the remedial course necessary.

Despite all, the Lord will respond to the one who responds to Him. There will be mutuality; He will sup with them and they with. Him, 3. 20; John 14. 23 compared with Luke 24. 29, 30 exemplify this. And this is where we are today. Christ is outside the professing religious system of Christianity, inside which all the fundamentals of the faith are denied despite the solemn oath given to defend and propagate them. Stipends are received despite the fact that the agreed services are not rendered. Such a breach of trust is almost incredible. But the Lord appeals to the individual – the mass is hopeless.

The overcomer is promised a place with Christ in His throne as also He Himself overcame and had sat down with His Father in His throne. Rev. 3. 21. Thus the Lord is at the right hand of God in heaven now, but later He will have His own throne on earth, and the overcomer will reign with Him, 2 Tim. 2. 12.

Conclusion. As he has penned these notes on the seven letters, the writer has felt how many by-paths there are which should have been explored profitably; yet to have done so would have protracted them too much. The reader is, however, urged to do this for himself. There are also not a few things difficult to be understood. We should wait upon the Lord for further light, not being negligent to examine the word diligently so that we may discover those things which have escaped us. The cross-references to Old Testament history and prophecies will yield much instruction if patiently traced out. May the Lord graciously grant that the few hints given may serve to stimulate further enquiry into these historic, prophetic, and practical letters.

Things Hereafter

A NEW SCENE

REVELATION 4, 5

IN INTERPRETING the book of the Revelation, it would seem that human logic must not be our guide. What heresy was wrought in using this method regarding the Person of Christ, whereby was invented the phrase 'the mother of God'. The present writer is quite well aware that some of the things which he will propound may appear to be illogical but he submits that they should not, therefore, be dismissed. The Spirit of God seems to present things in such a way that our spiritual sense overrides our mental deductions. This will be pointed out as we proceed and the reader must weigh the matter for himself.

In chapters 4 and 5 everything is different from what we have hitherto been considering. Things have changed.

THE TIMES ARE CHANGED. This is indicated in the phrase 'things which must come to pass hereafter', Rev. 4. 1 RV. The word 'hereafter' is precisely the same as in 1. 19 and means literally 'after these things'. We are here clearly in times after the history of Christendom has run its course, the true having been transferred to heaven and the false having been spewed out of His mouth. The church is not again seen on earth in this book till it reappears with Christ in chapter 19.

THE POSITION IS CHANGED. John is in heaven (see vv. 1, 2), and no longer on earth. The scenes of these two chapters are altogether heavenly.

Moreover, the THRONE IS CHANGED and what is now 'throne of grace', Heb. 4. 16, will at that time have become a throne of judgement out of which swift lightning-like judgements will proceed, being the 'voice' of God to men, thunderously reminding one of the dreadful times that accompanied the first giving of the law of Moses, Exod. 19; Heb. 12. 18-21.

THE SPIRIT, TOO, WILL HAVE CHANGED His ways. Not that this impugns the immutability of the Persons of the Godhead, but rather it recognizes an alteration in the manner of His dealing with men because the times will have changed. Instead of being a 'Spirit of grace', Heb. 10. 29, He will then be a Spirit of judgement fierce as burning lamps of fire.

There are, moreover, CHANGED CONDITIONS for hitherto, ever since the Lord visited the synagogue at Nazareth, the book has been closed by Him, Luke 4. 20, and the message of grace has been given to His servants to proclaim. He, having taken His seat at God's right hand, awaits expectantly the day when the same book is to be opened by Him, see Heb. 10. 13. Here in this chapter we see the book opened, introducing the events connected with the 'day of vengeance of our God' at which point the Lord, long ago, ceased to read. The 'acceptable year of the Lord' will then be over: the 'day of vengeance' will then have come.

But more, THE LAMB WILL HAVE CHANGED – not essentially but administratively. He will then have become the Lion, roaring, tearing, crushing His foes. All these changes characterize the book from chapter 6 onwards, though the change is observed to be in heaven, once John (a representative man) has been translated there. It is from heaven that the judgements are poured out on men on earth.

There is a throne set in heaven. Earth's thrones have been unstable, not firmly set, oftentimes overturned, and frequently vacant; rulers either have been assassinated or else they have abdicated. But heaven's throne is eternal, immovable, and unceasingly occupied. The Occupant appears as the first and the last colours of the breastplate, such are His multiple glories. The prepositions used in relation to the throne should be carefully noted, UPON the throne there is an Occupant. ROUND ABOUT the throne there is the rainbow, reminding us of God's pledge to His creature man which will not be broken, Gen. 9. 13. Also

ROUND ABOUT the throne are twenty-four thrones (not 'seats') occupied by twenty-four elders who are clothed in white with golden victor's crowns on their heads. These are the 'overcomers', those who have endured affliction and who will reign with Christ, 2 Tim. 2. 12. These remind us of the twenty-four priestly courses arranged by David, 1 Chr. 24. 4-5, 18, before Solomon occupied the throne. So here the elders are seen before Christ occupies His throne of rule on earth. They are the overcomers of whom we have already spoken, for they are clothed in white and wear golden victor's crowns, see Rev. 2. 10; 3. 11. OUT OF the throne there proceed lightnings and voices and thunders. BEFORE the throne are seven lamps of burning fire. And also BEFORE the throne is a glassy sea clear as crystal, in contrast to the wicked today who are like the restless sea casting up mire and dirt, Isa. 57. 20. There everything is tranquil, still, clear, and pure.

IN THE MIDST of the throne and ROUND ABOUT the throne are four living ones (not wild beasts) respectively like a lion, a calf, the face of a man and a flying eagle, after the fourfold division of the animal creation. The present writer suggests that these speak of the divine attributes as manifested in the Lord Jesus as presented in the four Gospels: Matthew as the Lion-King, Mark as the Calf-Servant, Luke as the Perfect Man and John as the Son of God who belongs to heaven, who is from heaven and is in heaven, consistent with the Lord Jesus calling Himself the 'Living One', *Zoon*, Rev. 1. 18. He is seen here in a fourfold aspect as 'Living Ones' – *Zoa* (the word 'creature' should not be in the translation; it is inaccurate and misleading). This may seem incompatible with 5. 6, but it is suggested that the chief characteristic of the Lord Jesus, the central feature, is that of a Lamb, and all four Gospels, irrespective of their peculiar traits, direct our attention to, and find their climax in, the slaying of the Lamb. The reader is referred to the preceding remarks regarding 'logic' in interpreting this book.

The Living Ones are full of eyes before and behind, for the Lord Jesus is omniscient, knowing all that has been and will be. And this accords with 5. 6 where the Lamb is seen to have 'seven horns and seven eyes', perfect power and perfect knowledge – almighty and omniscient. His inseparable identity with the Spirit of God surely shows how human logic cannot interpret these symbols of the Persons of the Godhead. All three Persons of the Godhead are inseparable each from the other though distinguishable in their activities.

The symbolic beings are full of eyes round about and within, and are equipped wing-like for instant activity to promote the glory of God. It was and is ever the business of the Lord Jesus to glorify the Father and time and again when here on earth He affirmed that He had not come to do His own will but the will of Him that sent Him (see e.g., John 17. 1, 4). In speaking of the Persons of the Godhead and their respective activities and their inter-relations we must not allow human intellect to guide. Logic fails us here, 'No heart but by Thy Spirit taught' can appreciate these things.

Heaven is here seen to be a place where there is both praise and weeping. Weeping in heaven! Well there may be, were the quest of the apostle John utterly and finally hopeless. Weeping occurs because it appears that truth is always to be on the gallows and evil is endlessly to triumph, seeing that none can be found to open the closed and sealed title deeds and to bring iniquity to a halt. But at last He who closed the book is identified as He who has triumphed to open the book. John is told that the Lion of the tribe of Judah has prevailed to do so, but when he turns he sees, not a lion but, a little lamb as it had been slain. Yet instead of lying dead on the ground it was standing: evidently it had come to life again. This tells of Christ, the Lamb of God, who had been slain at Calvary but raised again the third day and invested with all authority in heaven and earth, Matt. 28. 18. He is the eternal One, as the root of David existing before Him, and as his offspring coming after him. He is at once Deity and Humanity inseparably and eternally united from Bethlehem. Not only do we, as believers represented by the elders, worship the Lamb, but all the various facets in which the synoptic Gospels present the Lord Jesus contribute to add glory to Him as the Lamb foreknown, indeed, before the foundation of the world but manifested in these last times, the Centre of the church's worship and the Object of heaven's praise.

These two chapters record four paeans of praise in heaven: (1) by the living beings, 4. 8; (2) by the elders, 4. 11; (3) by the living ones plus the elders, 5. 8, and (4) by many angels, plus the living ones and the elders, 5. 11. In 5. 13 there is now achieved what God intended should be, Phil. 2. 10, and the whole universe bows in worship as there is the manifestation of the Father having glorified the Son and the Son having glorified the Father.

The various items of verse 12, power, wisdom, riches, might, honour, glory, and blessing are the eternal antitheses of all that the Lord Jesus temporarily experienced when on earth. Ponder this in detail, it will touch the heart. We do not elaborate here save to enumerate weakness, 2 Cor. 13. 4, the accusation of madness, John 10. 20, poverty, 2 Cor. 8. 9, meekness, Matt. 11. 29, shame, Heb. 12. 2, dishonour, Isa. 53. 3, and curse, Gal. 3. 13, as the things which were either said of Him or endured by Him when here. Thank God it is all over long since, but the issues flowing from them remain.

THE SEVEN SEALS

REVELATION 6, 7

THE CONTENTS of chapters 6 to 16 relate to the seals, trumpets and vials, and in each case there are seven. After the citing of the six seals, there is a parenthesis before the seventh is mentioned. The same applies to the trumpets. In interpreting these, it is necessary to discriminate between what is literal and what is symbolic. It would appear that where the literal meaning yields sense that should be regarded as what is intended.

Some have interpreted these historically as having already passed into history, either remote or less remote. Others regard them as having their fulfilment throughout the whole of time, the present being included. For our part, and for reasons already given, we relate all of them to the future. If there are parallels in ancient and modern history, it is because the same causes have the same effects at all times. Cause and effect are the same wherever such processes are at work. Evil always results in judgement. The advance of man's scientific achievements and technological advances does not affect the principles. It but affords a new sphere in which they operate. Any preliminary and partial apparent fulfilment of these various judgements is only because sin and its inevitable judgement are inseparably linked at all times.

It would seem that the seventh seal is not co-terminous with the seventh trumpet but that the seventh trumpet and the seventh vial are co-terminous. The 'mystery of God' is finished and 'the kingdoms of this world are become the kingdoms of our Lord, and of his Christ', 10. 7; 11. 15, is the grand goal and outcome of all that here transpires.

There is a wonderful harmony between the Olivet discourse as recorded by Matthew, Mark, and Luke (their own differences not being overlooked) and the prophetic forecasts of Paul in 2 Thessalonians 2 and of Peter in 2 Peter 3. It would unduly prolong these notes were we to deal at length and in detail with such items, but the Bible student should do this for himself if he is to gain confirmatory insight into the operation of the one Spirit of God in all three human penmen.

The seven seals first present to us four horsemen, 6. 2-8. The first appears to be that of an almost irresistible conqueror. To identify him is not easy. He appears to be one who ruthlessly drives his victorious car apparently without open war.

He is followed by the rider on the red horse. This speaks of civil war, internecine strife, mutual homicide.

The third is the black horse, telling of what inevitably follows such unsettled conditions, namely food having risen to famine prices. In the mercy of God the oil and the wine are not affected. We must bear in mind eastern conditions and not interpret these verses by our western mode.

76

The fourth is the pale horse and God's four sore judgements are then abroad in the earth, Ezek. 14. 21.

If our interpretation of the Living Ones is correct, namely that they speak of the Lord Jesus, how solemn is all this here! It is He who *now* invites the sinner to come to Him and find rest, and it is He who will *then* call for these judgements to 'come' (see RV reading throughout) and wreak their havoc among men. It is not that he invites John to 'come and see', KJV; rather He calls for the judgements to 'come', RV.

The fifth seal relates to those martyrs who had forfeited their lives rather than deny their faith. Following our interpretation of the book, this cannot relate to Christian martyrs, either past or present. All these, together with living saints, will have been raised and/or changed and 'caught up' to meet the Lord in the air prior to any of these happenings. They will be the seated and enthroned elders. The martyrs here alluded to under this fifth seal are post-rapture saints, absent from the body, present with the Lord, awaiting their resurrection, conscious, able to address Him and to be assured that all is under His loving and intelligent control and, in due course, that He would intervene on their behalf and the behalf of their fellow-servants and brethren. This affords a very instructive insight into conditions after death and before resurrection of the departed saints. It speaks of the intermediate state.

The sixth seal brings the darkening of the sun and the bloodlike transformation of the moon and the great earthquake, see Isa. 24. 13. This seems to be the ultimate fulfilment of Joel's prophecy quoted by Peter in Acts 2. 19, 20. It is, as the present writer believes, an utter mistake to link this with the three hours of darkness when the Lord died, or with the earthquake that followed. The time of it as given in Matthew 24. 29 forbids this, for it is immediately after the tribulation of those days. This is a yet-to-be terrible shaking by the hand of the Lord that spreads frantic anxiety among all, great and small, and an imagination (though they were wrong in fact) that the end of all things had come. There seems to be here a mixture of the literal and the symbolic. There is a world-wide upheaval, and the leading lights among men are cast down and their counsels are darkened. They are quite aware of a Superior Power at work among them which is adverse to all that they have encouraged. They seek to hide from the face of the One who sits on the throne and from the wrath of the Lamb. Ponder carefully the phrase 'the wrath of the Lamb' and all such subsequent similar phrases where the word 'Lamb' occurs. Who has known an angry lamb? The lamb-like character of our Saviour must not be allowed to nullify His stern qualities of justice and truth.

Before the seventh seal is opened there is a parenthesis in chapter 7, in which two parties are seen: (1) the sealed (i.e. those marked out as divinely owned and secure) from the twelve tribes of Israel (we feel that Manasseh should be Dan seeing that Joseph, the father of both Manasseh and Ephraim is mentioned) and (2) the numberless multitude from all sections of humanity. At the end of chapter 6 the question is asked, 'Who is able to stand?' RV, and here in chapter 7 there is a host of men and angels standing before the throne and before the Lamb. They have 'come out of the tribulation, the great one' (see Matt. 24. 21), not merely tribulation but a specific and recognized unequalled period of trouble. Delivered, washed, protected, satisfied, and comforted, their sorrows lay all behind them.

It is acknowledged that this poses great problems, but no greater than those which are raised by a satisfactory interpretation of many Old Testament prophecies, such as those which Ezekiel 37 involves. To these we may not at the moment have any satisfactory answer, but we may be assured that God will, in His own time and way, restore His earthly people Israel and do all that is here envisaged.

It may well be that the sealed of Israel will be the preachers of Matthew 24. 14 and that the vast number of those who stand before the Lamb are their converts. For if such great results were effected with but twelve apostles in Pentecostal times, how much greater when there are 144,000 available for this large evangelistic work?

It would NOT appear to be tenable that the events of Revelation 6 onwards follow *immediately* upon the rapture. So far as the present writer knows we are given no clue as to the length of time that will ensue between the translation of the saints to heaven and the commencement of Daniel's seventieth week. It is profitless to guess. But this evangelistic work will go on in the end time.

SEVEN TRUMPETS

REVELATION 8

WHEN THE SEVENTH SEAL is opened there is silence in heaven for half an hour, portending the oncoming of further calamities. The seven trumpets are about to be sounded, but we are informed in symbolic language that what will transpire then will be in response to the prayers of the saints, 8. 3-5. The present-day characteristic is that we should pray for our enemies, and, as did the Lord and as Stephen, seek their forgiveness. But in days yet to come, the so-called imprecatory psalms will then be the appropriate prayer of God's people calling for judgement. By these trumpets those prayers will be answered. We must distinguish the various periods in the ways of God. *Now* it is the day of His grace and our prayers should be regulated accordingly. *Then* it will be the 'day of vengeance' and their prayers will be suited to such a time.

Why it should be the fourth part of the earth elsewhere, 6. 8, but in these trumpets only third parts occur, 8. 7-12, eludes us. We know what has been said by others, but proof appears to be lacking. How much of these trumpet judgements is literal and how much is symbolic we must leave our readers each to decide for himself. A great mountain may allude to some mighty kingdom in the world. A great star may refer to some individual person who is a leading light among men. But it is worth considering that, as at the beginning, the solar system became chaotic and God restored it to order in the space of six days, so later on there will be chaotic conditions in the actual heavens, sun, moon and stars all being affected. Does 8. 12 explain how the 'days will be shortened', Matt. 24. 22? Many questions can be asked which are less easily answered.

In this connection, the phrase 'them that dwell upon the earth', is a phrase of very frequent occurrence (3. 10; 6. 10; 8. 13; 11. 10; 12. 12; 13. 8, 12, 14; 14. 6; 17. 2, 8). It relates to those who settle down here on earth as if it were their permanent dwelling place. How awful are the woes that befall such! Compare with this Phil. 3. 19.

THREE WOES

REVELATION 9, 10

THREE WOES follow. We read of the first in 9. 1-11. It relates to a terrible darkening influence caused apparently by released evil spirits that come up from the pit of the abyss, devastating as locusts, the threat of war hanging over men causing unceasing fear. 'Hair as the hair of women', v. 8, may show that they are all compulsorily subject to a mighty power (see 1 Cor. 11. 3, 15), who is a king, the angel of the abyss, Abaddon (Hebrew), Apollyon (Greek) meaning in each case Destroyer.

The 'tails' may refer to the false prophets, if by analogy we are justified in referring to Isaiah 9. 15. God's own sealed ones are providentially secure. Five months is said to be the life of a certain species of locust. In our own times we have known the terror, the fear, the frustration which come from the threat of war in this or that part of the earth. So it will be then but on an enhanced scale. There will be no light upon the situation; all the world rulers will be utterly confounded not knowing what to do. That the foreboding threat will materialize is certain, shown by what follows.

The second woe follows. It is apparent that God is over all, holding things back till His time has come, for He has His hour, His day, His month, and His year. Earth's rulers may plan but the counsel of the Lord will stand. When His hour comes, His judgement will strike. Read 9. 13-21, and note how He who sits in the heavens controls all in every detail, making the wrath of man to praise Him. Yet, however much His judgements come upon men, those who escape with their lives do not repent of their sins, whether those sins be against God, v. 20, or against man, v. 21.

It is not till we reach 11. 14 that the second woe is past, so we must consider chapter 10 and the early part of chapter 11 to be parenthetical (a characteristic feature of this part of the book). The 'mighty angel' of 10. 1 would appear to be the Lord Jesus Himself in this particular role. He is the angel of the covenant, so frequently mentioned in the Old Testament. The 'cloud' speaks of divine glory; cp. the pillar of cloud in the wilderness. The 'rainbow' signifies His faithfulness. The 'sun' denotes His life-giving, healing, and warming strength; cp. Mal. 4. 2. The 'fire' is emblematic of judgement. The 'sea' speaks of the nations. The 'earth' in all likelihood refers to Israel signified by their 'land' (the word 'earth' may be rendered 'land'). The 'little book' (a diminutive of a diminutive) denotes the title deeds asserting the rights of the Lord Jesus, and the time is now come when He will forcibly claim them. He appears in the role of a roaring lion (see notes on ch. 5). In 6. 10 the martyrs enquire 'How long?', and here the Claimant with one foot planted on the land and one on the sea affirms that there shall be delay no longer, 10. 6 RV marg. He is about to claim His rights. Then God's hidden secret, 'the mystery of God', will be finished, and the kingdoms of this world will be wrenched from the hand of the usurper; cp. Luke 4. 6; and they will become manifestly those of our Lord and His Christ, Rev. 11. 15. Then will be answered the prayer, 'Thy kingdom come', Matt. 6. 10.

But the route thither will not be easy or pleasant as John knew. It is one thing to have these prophecies 'in my mouth' where they are pleasant to taste, but another thing altogether to enter into them in one's innermost being. How easy it is glibly to talk of prophetic matters! How solemn it is to enter into all that is entailed when they are implemented!

Chapter 11 deals with the temple and then with that which is outside the temple. It would appear that it relates to the time when Israel is back in the land, and when there will be in Jerusalem that which is very similar to the Vatican enclosure within the city of Rome nowadays – a literal, visible, tangible temple.

Here we read of 'forty and two months', and 'a thousand two hundred and threescore days', each being identical with a period of three and a half years, and also with 'a time, and times, and half a time', 12. 14. A Bible year is made up of 360 days as will appear by consulting Gen. 7. 11, 24; 8. 4, and this period refers apparently to the second half of the last week of Daniel's famous heptad prophecy, Dan. 9. 24-27. A proper understanding of this important prophecy seems essential to a proper understanding of the prophetic scriptures generally, and this book of the Revelation not less than others.

THE TWO WITNESSES

REVELATION 11

THE PRESENT WRITER is not prepared categorically to affirm the identity of the two witnesses spoken of in chapter 11. In Zechariah 4 they were Joshua and Zerubbabel, the high priest and the governor. But the things wrought by the two witnesses of Revelation 11 are reminiscent of what Moses and Elijah did in their day, for the former turned water into blood and the latter called fire down from heaven, Exod. 7. 19; 2 Kgs. 1. 10. But since it is appointed unto men

'once' to die, and since Moses died, there is not a little to be said for the suggestion that Moses may not be referred to, but that these witnesses may be Enoch and Elijah neither of whom died, but each was translated to heaven without death. Moreover, Enoch was not of Israel for that nation had not then been called, and Elijah was; thus we have here the testimony to all the world in its twofold division – Jews and Gentiles.

Yet again, we may ask if the number two is merely symbolic of an adequate testimony and is not to be limited to two specific persons. 'At the mouth of two witnesses . . . shall the matter be established', Deut. 19. 15; John 8. 17. If so, they might represent two companies. Whether individuals or classes of individuals they are plainly reservoirs of divine power (olive trees) and divine testimony (two lampstands). They certainly are Moses-like and Elijah-like, for they have power over the waters to turn them into blood, and they have power to shut heaven that it rain not during the time of their prophecy.

Another person now appears in verse 7 called 'the beast that cometh up out of the abyss', RV. He wars against the witnesses and kills them. Who is the beast? He is a 'wild beast' and appears to be the head of the revived Roman empire, or, indeed, it may refer to the empire itself. For the word 'beast' is used in the Apocalypse in both senses. It evidently has had an existence, and then had disappeared and now reappears. This is true to fact touching the Roman empire which once existed and now does not exist, though attempts for its resuscitation are being frantically made. The scene of his opposition and apparent but short-lived triumph over this testimony is Jerusalem so significantly described in verse 8: Sodom-like for its moral corruption, Egypt-like for its cruel violence, indisputably the Jerusalem of Palestine where our Lord was crucified. The reading of this verse certainly seems to favour the notion that two persons are in view and not two classes.

Maybe we shall have to wait till the time comes to see the literal fulfilment of this section which seems so clouded with difficulties at the moment.

With the sounding of the seventh trumpet, the counsels of God in regard to the kingdoms of this world will have been achieved. It is to be noted that the words 'and art to come' should not appear in verse 17, RV. There is simply 'which art, and wast', because by this time the Lord will have come. Then Psalm 2. 5 and Psalm 110. 5 will have come to pass.

The judgement in verse 18 does not relate to the great white throne judgement but 'the time of the dead (to) be judged' refers more appropriately to Revelation 6. 10, and has to do with the vindication of those who were unjustly condemned by men. It is an earthly scene whereas the judgement of 20. 11ff. is when heaven and earth have fled away. This is the great clash between hostile man and God against whom man has set himself. The victory is in no doubt. Note that 11. 19 should be joined to chapter 12.

Thus verses 15 to 18 take us right on to the end, the glorious triumph of God's Christ over His enemies, the vindication of His own, many of whom have suffered martyrdom, and the establishment of His kingdom on earth. From chapter 12 to chapter 16 we are given details of events that must transpire before that time comes.

THE MAN CHILD

REVELATION 12

CHAPTER 12 HAS TO DO with two matters, (1) the persecution of God's faithful Israelite remnant and (2) the ejection of the devil from heaven. The woman is the nation of Israel from whom, according to the flesh, Christ came, Rom. 9. 5. He is the 'man child'. The 'dragon' is the devil.

The woman is seen arrayed with the sun and the moon is under her feet, depicting, it would appear, God's original intention concerning Israel that that nation was to be the leading light, and all others were to be beneath them. The crown of twelve stars might speak of her twelve tribes and her administrative authority. The time of travail here depicted seems to indicate the great tribulation through which she is yet to pass; cp. Jer. 4. 31; 6. 23, 24; 30. 7; Matt. 24. 21. But let this be carefully observed that the first and the second advents of Christ are here telescoped, for we believe that the second is envisaged in verse 2 when Christ will come and bring to an end Israel's trouble in the future, and verse 5 envisages His past advent when He was born in Bethlehem. The woman certainly cannot be the Virgin Mary to whom the features cited did not apply. Romans 9. 5 shows that Israel is Christ's national mother.

The great red dragon is likewise depicted as he will be later, the unseen power energizing the revived Roman empire which had been marked by seven imperialistic forms of government and is yet to be revived under an eighth, to whom ten kings will give their allegiance. (We consider this later). The whole thing is wrapped together in one small compass, time being ignored, the first and second advents being joined together in one panel. There can be no doubt that the man child of verse 5 is the Lord Jesus Christ, though the words 'caught up' seem to echo 1 Thessalonians 4. 17, and this linked with 2. 27 of our book seems to imply that Christ and the church are conjointly in view, Christ at His ascension and the church at the rapture.

Ignoring time, the woman, that is the godly remnant of Israel, flees into the wilderness where she is nourished for twelve hundred and sixty days, the last half of Daniel's seventieth week as we have seen. There she will have a 'pavilion' prepared for her preservation and Psalm 46 will be her consoling experience. It is important to note how the whole of the era from Pentecost to the rapture is passed over in this panel of truth. This is often the way of prophecy, and failure to grasp this feature is responsible for many fantastic interpretations of prophecy in general and this one in particular. We cannot stay to deal with them here. Let the reader rather judge the foregoing suggestions for himself.

The 'war in heaven', Rev. 12. 7, does *not follow* these events as will be apparent from verse 14 where the period called 'a time, and times, and half a time' is identical with the twelve hundred and sixty days. Verses 7 to 11 go into details that are not dealt with in verses 1 to 6 and which account for the devil's activities on earth at that time.

Michael is Israel's special prince in the spiritual realm looking after her national interests; see Dan. 12. 1. The identification of the devil under his various names. Rev. 12. 9, shows him to be the intruder into Eden's garden. He is also the one who appears before

God in Job 1 and 2, and in Zechariah 3. 1. He is the accuser of the brethren.

> Though the restless foe accuses,
> Sins recounting like a flood:
> Every charge our God refuses,
> Christ has answered with His blood.

> I hear the accuser roar
> Of ills that I have done;
> I know them well and thousands more,
> Jehovah findeth none.

Let the reader ponder carefully Zechariah 3; Romans 8. 31ff; John 13. 10; 1 John 4. 17. Satan is the *dragon* in the sea causing its unrest and disturbance, Isa. 27. 1. He is the old *serpent* supreme in devilish wisdom. He is the *devil*, the great slanderer; *Satan*, the great adversary of God and man; the *deceiver* of the nations leading them blindly on to follow him to perdition.

His ejection from heaven is the initial step to the establishment of Messiah's kingdom on earth, Rev. 12. 10. 'How long?', 6. 10, is answered by 'Delay no longer', Rev. 10. 6 RV marg., and now his time is 'short', 12. 12. Things are on the march.

Violent attempts will be made by the devil to destroy God's earthly people, but without success. 'Water as a flood' may be compared with Isaiah 10. 26; 28. 2, 15; 59. 19. But God's providential care of His people and His defeat of their opponents, signified by the earth opening her mouth and swallowing up the river, will effect their final deliverance.

It will be noted that John frequently takes us to the end, and then goes back reviewing other things that lead to the same goal. Therefore many items run concurrently. Through it all God has a loyal and faithful remnant, in the minority, marked by constancy in testimony to the Lord Jesus and in obedience to God's word. It is this that gives them patience and stimulates their faith; see Rev. 12. 17;

13. 10. We should not allow our pre-occupation with prophetic matters so to absorb us that these practical lessons are overlooked. Prophecy was given to promote godliness, not to encourage or satisfy curiosity.

TWO WILD BEASTS

REVELATION 13

CHAPTER 13 BRINGS before us two great leaders of the last days, the one coming up from the sea (symbolic of international unrest) and the other out of the earth (land) that is the land of Palestine. The utterly confused and disturbed state of mankind will furnish the dragon with his golden opportunity to bring forward his superman, the great political head of the revived Roman empire, the claimant of divine honours. His seat will be in Rome, Rev. 17. 18. He will be one of a blasphemous trinity, consisting of the dragon, the first wild beast, and the second wild beast, all answering to and mimicking the three persons of the Holy Trinity. As the Lord Jesus promoted the glory of the Father so, too, the second beast will take steps to see that man worships the first beast, 13. 12. It is ever the devil's way to caricature and imitate what God does. There are the 'deep things' of the Spirit, and Satan has his deep things. Christ has his bride and the devil brings forward his whore, or harlot. There is the Holy Trinity and the devil is one of a corrupt trinity. There are the true apostles, and the devil has his false apostles.

We can in our present day appreciate the craving of mankind for a superman who can take in hand human affairs and administer them better than has hitherto been done. All prior efforts have but resulted in confusion being made the more confounded. Man has not been able to deal with the factor that is the cause of all the trouble, namely, sin. Satan will make a supreme and final attempt. He will have his man. Maybe he will be Nero raised from the dead. Who knows? Does 17. 8 imply this? *Nero redivivus* was frequently and for long spoken of. Men nearer to his time expected him to come back.

The first wild beast will embody all the elements of the four former great empires spoken of by Daniel, first seen as a great magnifical image, Dan. 2, and later as four ravenous beasts, Dan. 7. All these beasts reappear here. This final revived empire will comprise elements and principles of all that has preceded. Ten kings will yield their power to him for one hour, namely for a term of seven years. These are the ten horns of verse 1. He will be the eighth of a series of seven preceding forms of imperial government, yet one of the seven. Just as all authority has been given to the Lord Jesus by the Father, Matt. 28. 18, so the dragon imitates God and gives this beast his power and throne and great authority. Everything will be apparently so similar to what God has done, even imitating a sacrificial slaying and subsequent resurrection, Rev. 13. 14, so that the very elect might be deceived. The reader should consult Daniel 7. 11, 20 and 2 Thessalonians 2. 4; these verses surely will convince the reader that the person there alluded to is the same as the first beast here. Like Nebuchadnezzar, he will have worldwide authority. He will defy not only all men but heaven itself. He will persecute and overcome the saints. If ever there was a time that calls for 'faith and patience' it will be then. This is the deification of the imperial power and the demand for its universal recognition and worship, a thing known in John's day and a thing yet to be seen in the not distant future. His will be absolute, autocratic rule with no mercy.

He will be aided and abetted by a second wild beast, Rev. 13. 11. This appears to be the 'idol shepherd' of Zechariah 11. 17, the wilful king of Daniel 11. 36, and the 'other that comes in his own name' of John 5. 43. There is so much that is common to each of these beasts (they being characteristically alike), that they are often confused. But this second wild beast caricatures the Lamb of God and is willingly subservient to, and seeks the honour and worship of, the first beast. He will operate in Jerusalem as the first does in Rome. The 'image', which at his instigation is erected to him in the temple at Jerusalem, appears to be identical with 'the abomination' that maketh desolate of Matthew 24. 15 and Mark 13. 14, and it is by this image that the beast sits in the temple of God setting himself forth as God, 2 Thess. 2. 4 RV. In fact the reader should compare verses 13 and 14 of our chapter with 2 Thessalonians 2. 9, 10, where miracle working and deception are found in each section.

The 'mark', imitative of the 'sealing' of Revelation 7. 3, and the general boycott are all too plainly stated to need comment. God seals on the forehead, for there is nothing clandestine with Him, but the devil's mark may be either in forehead or in hand, seen or unseen. It is imperative, however, that it be in one place or the other. As to the number of his name, the most that we will say is that six is the number of imperfection, as seven is that of perfection. Here is a threefold cord of consummate imperfection in a man who devotes himself to bringing the whole world into allegiance to the devilish trinity. Many, many conjectures have been made as to the meaning of this number, and many names have been assigned to it. We think in all cases wrongly, because it plainly relates to a person yet to appear in the future. But there are many significant mentions of the numeral six, either singly or triply, in the Old Testament which are worth while searching out.

This, of course, denotes both political and religious rule seen in the respective two beasts, a combination frequently noted in scripture and operative in the world throughout its ages down to the present time. This involves both Jew and Gentile, Jerusalem and Rome. Capital punishment will be meted out to those who refuse to bow to the state and ascribe to it the honours due to God alone. Humanitarianism, while it may pretend to exist in the case of civil and moral crimes, will not be admitted when it is a matter of what will then be 'religious conviction' and personal 'faith'. But God will even then have those as of old who are willing to brave the fiery furnace and the lions' den rather than concede to such heartless and blasphemous demands.

Times like these existed in John's day. Times like them exist somewhere on earth in our day. But the full development of these unequalled and never-to-be-repeated times of terror and intolerance lies yet in the future. It will be for forty and two months; a time, times, and half a time; three and a half years; twelve hundred and sixty days; the last half of Daniel's seventieth week.

The doom of the beasts is considered in chapter 19.

SIX ANGELS

REVELATION 14

IN THE BEGINNING of chapter 14, we are brought to the consummation of God's purposes as set out in Psalm 2. 5. The Lord Jesus and the Israelite remnant are now given their earthly rights. The Lamb and the one hundred and forty-four thousand are together on mount Zion, whose establishment and history under David is set out in the Old Testament. They are, as it seems (though some demur) identical with those in chapter 7, and it speaks of the triumphant victory of the godly remnant of Israel under their Messiah, viewed here as the Lamb. They are in harmony with heaven and, having this altogether new experience, they sing the new song. Their character is described: they are virgins, cp. Matt. 25. 1ff.; undefiled, S. of S. 5. 2; they follow the Lamb wherever He goes as His retinue; they have been redeemed; they are a firstfruits because, as we saw in chapter 7, there is a vast host other than they; they are 'without fault'. They are the only ones on earth who are able to learn the heavenly song.

Thereafter we are shown the activities of a series of angels, reminding us of the Lord's explanatory words, 'the reapers are the angels', Matt. 13. 39. The first has the 'everlasting gospel', for it certainly is good news to know that God will intervene in judgement on behalf of His own and in suppression of His and their foes, vv. 6-7. His present silence perplexes not a few, and calls for the exercise of faith on the part of all.

The second angel declares as accomplished the inevitable doom of Babylon, v. 8, of which John has yet much to say in chapters 17 and 18.

The third tells of the penalty to be paid for worshipping the beast and his image. (How this must have encouraged the people both in John's day and in the later dark ages where there was so much demand for emperor worship, vv. 9-12.)

The fourth angel declares the 'harvest of the earth', v. 15, while the sixth applies his sickle to the 'vine', v. 18. Judgement is worldwide, both on Gentiles (the earth) and on Israel (the vine). The Lord Jesus had been in the winepress of Gethsemane and suffered outside of the wall of Jerusalem. As a retributive judgement, Israel will go through the winepress which will be trodden outside the city. The mileage is given as sixteen hundred furlongs, namely, what we would call two hundred miles. Everything is retributive in verses 18 to 20, the murder of God's Son being avenged at the hands of the nation that was guilty thereof. Had not their forebears said, 'His blood be on us, and on our children', Matt. 27. 25? Consider Psalm 29 for the length of the battle line, from Lebanon in the north to Kadesh in the south. God's longsuffering waits until the harvest is 'over-ripe', Rev. 14. 15 RV. In verse 18 the 'altar' speaks of the cross, and the 'vine' of the nation of Israel; cp. Ps. 80. 8, 14 and Isa. 5. 1. The 'wrath' of God is His governmental judicial retributive actions on that people for their guilt at Calvary.

The whole scene of chapter 14 is panoramic, gathering up the loose threads and putting them together, showing the climax of things as to the remnant, vv. 1-5, as to earth-dwellers, vv. 6-7, as to Babylon, v. 8, as to the worshippers of the beast, vv. 9-12, as to martyrs, v. 13, as to mankind in general, vv. 14-16, and as to Israel in particular, vv. 17-20.

It should be stressed that we are confronted with the active wrath of God, 14. 19; 15. 1, 7, but the believer of the present calling is assured of immunity from it, 1 Thess. 1. 10; 5. 9; Rom. 5. 9; Rev. 3. 10. We have sought to make this clear in our earlier chapters.

SEVEN VIALS

REVELATION 15, 16

CHAPTER 15 FURNISHES US with preliminary scenes prior to the pouring out of the seven vials (or bowls). They are the last plagues by which the wrath of God will be finished. In verses 2-4 we are given a heavenly triumphant scene of singing. It is the song which Moses sang, a song that relates to the Lamb, and concerns the mighty, ultimate deliverance of God's people from Gentile bondage far worse than the original Egyptian bondage, and their acknowledgment of Israel's true King and Israel's national rights. In this connection read Psalm 22. 31; Isaiah 66. 23 and Zechariah 14. 18-19.

We are now given in chapter 16 details of the judgements of the seven vials poured out from heaven upon men. A careful comparison of these with the seven trumpets will show that they are developments of those trumpet judgements, similar things being found in each of them. They are the outworking of strictly righteous principles (cp. 15. 6 with 1. 13), and terrible though they may seem it is but meet that iniquity and cruelty should be rewarded appropriately. There is doubtless much in these judgements which should be read literally. Maybe some should be regarded symbolically. For example, the drying up of the Euphrates may well not be literal, but can be interpreted in the light of modern achievements which make the widest of rivers no insuperable barrier to oncoming armies. But we must ever be wary against bringing in modern inventions and conditions as a means of interpreting scripture, since they so quickly become outdated.

The similarity to the plagues in Egypt is patent, thus throwing light on the prophetic significance of Israel's historic bondage and deliverance. God will repeat on a proportionately large scale what man has repeated on a similar scale in regard to God's earthly people. 'True and righteous are thy judgments', 16. 7, true to His word and righteous in its principle. Man cannot complain of injustice for he is but receiving what he has merited. Judgement will then be as ever 'according to their works'. Seeing the Egyptian plagues were actual, why should not these vial judgements be actual also?

It is vainly hoped that when God intervenes in judgement man will repent of his sins. Two relatively recent great world wars have shown, however, that this is but wishful thinking, and groundless at that. Men only blaspheme God and do not repent of their ways.

The 'darkening' of the kingdom of the beast declares how all his policies, schemes, methods, and directives fail in attaining his designs. He is bewildered and knows not what to do. This is the fifth seal.

The 'kings of the east' mentioned next, 16. 12, are those eastern territories which lie outside the sphere covered by the revived Roman empire. The eastern peril has always and still does threaten the west, their limitless hordes spreading terror in the minds of men. Three unclean spirits like frogs come out of the mouth of this blasphemous and false trinity of iniquity (see our remarks on chapter 13) and thereby is precipitated the great clash of arms between east and west at Har-Magedon. A trinity of evil drives them to vocal decisions which spell their disaster. In the writer's view, Russia and her hordes will be dealt with later. Joel 3 should be read in connection with our chapter 16 as well as those passages in Isaiah which relate to the onslaughts of the Assyrian. This will result in the utter collapse of Gentile civilization and the western union. The 'great city', that is Jerusalem, Rev. 11. 8, as well as the other cities of the world, will fall. Babylon, the vast political and religious union of the western world, will collapse. This is the finishing of the wrath of God on men, 15. 1.

THE GREAT WHORE

REVELATION 17, 18

CHAPTER 17 IS ONE of the most important chapters in the whole book. It gives us particulars of the great whore (or as the RV renders the word, the 'great harlot'). Everything that man produces is 'great', the 'great harlot', 'Babylon the great', 'the great city' and so on frequently throughout the book.

She is a harlot, utterly abandoned, acknowledging no principles of purity and human rights. She is the dark sinister power behind the throne, as was Jezebel behind Ahab, and Herodias and her daughter behind Herod. Religious power is the hidden hand behind the political scene, holding the reins, directing, and controlling. Oppressively she sits on the waters, which are peoples, multitudes, nations and tongues, 17. 15. How crushingly burdensome is state religion! Satiated prelates exploit the people; they roll in wealth and the people, whom they hold in religious fear, wallow in poverty.

Kings derive their power from God: they are His servants, Rom. 13. 1ff., and they owe their loyalty to Him alone, but their illicit alliance with this harlot is spiritual 'fornication'. Peoples become infatuated with her as one drunken with wine.

In this chapter, we are in days when the beast is in control, yet not in control. He is ridden by the woman. That beast is the revived Roman empire which has seven heads and ten horns. The explanation of this is given in the chapter itself. The seven heads evidently represent seven imperialistic forms of power, once existent in a city founded on seven hills. As the Roman empire once existed, but does not now exist (though elements of it are to be found in the laws of the countries that once comprised it) so this beast was and is not, and is about to come out of the abyss. Doubtless modern-day trends betray a frantic endeavour to revive that former state of things, though it be not called that. Yet there is extant today the 'Treaty of Rome'.

Because of the plain words of scripture, the writer does not believe that the ancient city of Babylon will ever be rebuilt; see Jer. 50 and 51, and specially 51. 64. And not only so, but it has no hills; it is in the plain of Shinar. The word Babylon is symbolic of that Babel-like confusion of western civilization, dominated by a cruel beast-like monster, and that monster himself controlled by the dark sinister influence of the corrupt religious system of the world, the counterfeit of the true. We do not say that this is merely Roman Catholicism: doubtless it embodies that but it may well incorporate within its folds (and who cannot see the trend toward this in our own times) every other so-called Christian religious profession, which are her daughters. The woman is royally clad, Rev. 17. 4, for she claims divine honours, and has every indication of abundant wealth. Her abominations, that is, her idolatries, are notorious. She is drunken with the blood of the martyrs of Jesus, for she is an arch-persecutrix. This is the 'mystery of lawlessness', 2 Thess. 2. 7 RV, in its fully developed and final state. No marvel that John wonders; he certainly does not admire her, Rev. 17. 6, see KJV and RV.

Daniel 7. 24ff. sheds light on the ten kings who give their power to the beast for one hour. They are the ten toes of Daniel 2. 42 and the 'ten horns' of Daniel 7. 20. This 'hour' appears to be Daniel's final heptad. These kings make war with the Lamb but are overcome by Him.

But there is a further item put, it is suggested, not in chronological order (for Revelation 17. 14 occurs after 17. 16), namely that of the casting off of the woman from the beast and burning her with fire. That such things have transpired in past history is admitted, the times of Luther and the French Revolution being witness, but what is spoken of here is the final overthrow. This would make way for the erection of the image in the temple at Jerusalem, to which all must bow in unchallenged worship. While the woman was holding the reins it could hardly be that the image could be the sole claimant to religious allegiance.

Verse 18 identifies the city beyond doubt as Rome. She was at that time reigning with unopposed power.

We must not fail to glean spiritual and practical consolations from this sombre chapter. It is apparent from verse 17 that God is over all and that He operates even in circumstances which at the time appear to be so strange and so adverse to His glory. As God overruled the wicked acts of Joseph's brethren for their ultimate good, so God overrules the counsels of the kings of the earth in relation to the beast to the ultimate fulfilment of His will, v. 17.

If in chapter 17 we have the fall of religious Babylon, in chapter 18 we have the repercussions of that fall upon the commercial world. The vast monetary resources of ecclesiastical establishments are invested in commercial enterprises, and with the overthrow of the one is the calamity of the other. Of this chapter 18 speaks. The true church is a habitation of God by His Spirit, Eph. 2. 22, but Babylon will then have become a habitation of demons, and a hold of every unclean spirit and a hold of every unclean and hateful bird, Rev. 18. 2. This is what the tree of Christendom has grown to be, Matt. 13. 32. For what devilish idea and practice is not even now harboured under the guise of Christianity?

The 'merchants' of the earth have enriched themselves by her, but when her desolation comes they will weep and mourn. Twice this is said in Revelation 18. 11 and 15; their gain is at an end. That there are true people of God involved in this vast religious system one cannot doubt; we have met them. Oh that verse 4 were blazoned abroad so that all would take heed and obey! Oh that those who are outside would cease to fraternise with, and thereby encourage, those inside!

Verse 6 is the principle of rendering like for like, and the reader should consult Exodus 22. 9; Isaiah 40. 2 and Genesis 41. 32 for similar expressions. It is not spiteful vindictiveness (who could attribute this to God?), but the inevitable judgement that attaches to the proven sins. Verse 8 refers to 17. 16; these kings become God's instrument of judgement, they themselves confiscating as much of her wealth as they can digest.

The vast system is judged, a system which put 'gold' as of prime value and the 'souls of men' as of least significance. It is all brought about 'in one hour', 18. 17, for when God rises to judge who can resist Him? And He works speedily. It seems as though here God takes account of all her wicked and murderous activities and not merely those of the last times; see v. 24. Her whole record is brought to account and judgement meted out accordingly. It is the final overthrow of apostate Christendom, Rome and her daughters.

THE GRAND FINALE

REVELATION 19 to 21. 8

LITTLE NEED BE said about chapter 19, as we have surveyed much of it in our opening comments. The scene is in heaven which is full of Hallelujahs because of what has transpired on earth as set out in chapters 17 and 18. But the counterpart is seen. The chaste virgin, the true bride, is here seen in wedding array for 'the marriage of the Lamb' has come. Who is this bride? Surely none other than those of Ephesians 5. 27; none other than those who comprise under other imagery, the body of Christ, and the holy temple; see Eph. 1. 23; 2. 21. There are the guests who are 'called' to the wedding, and we suggest that these are Old Testament saints and post-rapture saints. The bridal attire has been wrought out by the bride, for 'the fine linen is the righteous acts of the saints', Rev. 19. 8 RV. She has made her own trousseau.

The Lord Jesus appears here not only as the Bridegroom but as the great Executor of God's judgements on earth. All judgement has been given to the Son, John 5. 22. With Him is the church which is not only seen as the bride but as those who share in the conquests and reign of the Bridegroom. Here in. verses 11 onwards we have, not the coming of the Lord *for* His people, but His coming *with* them to earth in judgement with which so much of the Old Testament and the synoptic Gospels have to do. Lest any think it inappropriate that the bride should share in this, let him consult Revelation 2. 27 which shows otherwise.

His enemies make war against Him but the beast and the false prophet, the first and second wild beasts. of chapter 13, are taken and cast alive into the lake of fire. Two men went to heaven without dying, namely Enoch and Elijah, while here two men go to hell without dying. Even at the end of the millennium they are still there; they will not have been annihilated. There is annihilation for none.

The rest are slain by His sword which came forth out of His mouth. It is the 'voice of the Lord' of Psalm 29. He has but to speak, and it is done.

Here is the very antithesis of Matthew 21. There the lowly king riding upon a colt enters Jerusalem and all are enquiring, 'Who is this?', v. 10. But here, is the same Person, a mighty Warrior riding a white horse, emblematic of retributive justice, with His name blazoned on His breast so that all knew His identity. It is no longer the time of 'his patience' but 'the day of his power'.

Thereafter the devil is incarcerated in the abyss for one thousand years. The abyss must be distinguished from 'the lake of fire', for from the latter there is no return, but there is from the former.

The first resurrection having been completed, Rev. 20. 5, the Lord Jesus assumes His crown rights and He reigns for a thousand years. Of course this is not the full extent of the term of His kingdom, for it is an everlasting kingdom and of it there shall be no end. But the term of a thousand years is introduced because it relates to the final probation of man under the most favourable of all conditions. We utterly fail to see how any can interpret this period but literally. As the world is now characterized by an absent Christ and a present devil, so then it will be the reverse. That period will be marked by a present Christ and an absent devil. It will be the time of 'regeneration', Matt. 19. 28,'times of refreshing', Acts 3. 19, 'the times of restitution of all things', Acts 3. 21. Nevertheless it will only serve to show that man is but flesh and that flesh is irremediable no matter what advantages man may be given. It cannot be altered. Therefore at the end of the thousand years the devil is released, and men flock to his standard in rebellion against the best king it has ever known or had. But the rebellion is short-lived and the issue is final and eternal.

It is better to read all this in the simplicity of faith. We see no reason to doubt that one thousand years means exactly that, and the other periods which we have had cause to mention also mean literally what they are called. And the notion that either the millennium is now running its course, or that there is no such thing as a time of millennial blessing yet to come, causes us to marvel that sane, not to say spiritual men, can entertain such thoughts. But they do!

The Lord Jesus is not now reigning, see 1 Cor. 4. 8, but the time of His reign will then have come, Rev. 19. 6, 16. At present he is God's King in reserve (see 2 Chr. 22. 11 for an Old Testament type of this), but then He will be God's King, first reigning in David-like fashion clearing the scene of His enemies and then establishing Solomon-like world-wide peace and prosperity. After the final doom of the devil spoken of in Revelation 20. 10, the fulfilment of 1 Corinthians 15. 24 will be seen.

Then follows the judgement of the great white throne, the supreme court of divine justice, from which there is no appeal. Verses 11 to 15 of chapter 20 should be pondered seriously, rejoicing in John 5. 24 and 1 John 4. 17, but bearing in mind our duty to spare no effort that we might 'by all means save some', 1 Cor. 9. 22.

The first eight verses of chapter 21 take us into the eternal state. As to these, the writer may refer the reader to his book *Concerning the Future*. As we are giving here but a brief survey of the Apocalypse, we shall not go into details beyond suggesting that those referred to in verse 3 may be those who have come through the millennium into the eternal state without dying.

All the damage wrought by the introduction of sin into the human race will then be undone. God will have triumphed and the devil will have been defeated. Darkness will not have overcome the

Light. Tears, death, sorrow, pain will all be things of the past. It will well repay study to compare the beginning of our Bible – Genesis 1 to 6 – with the end of the Revelation. The contrast is sharp and vivid.

THE BRIDE, THE LAMB'S WIFE

REVELATION 21. 9 – 22. 5

FROM VERSE 10 of chapter 21, we are given a description of the bride, the Lamb's wife who is likened to the holy city, the new Jerusalem, coming down from God out of heaven. It is as a spotlessly transparent luminary in the universe not needing either sun or moon for it enshrined the Shekinah glory of God. It had a protective wall so that nothing that defiled or made an abomination (idol) or a lie could enter thereinto. Only those whose names are in the Lamb's book of life could enter.

It had *twelve gates* which touched every point of the compass and on which were inscribed the names of the twelve tribes of Israel, for we believe that this is a millennial scene. Restored Israel is distinct from this city. In the eternal state all such distinctions do not exist. This city is central, and as oriental gates had names thereon indicating the road leading to the place named, so here. The order is the church, then Israel, then the nations. This holy city is the church of which Paul writes to the Ephesians that it is built upon the *foundation* of the apostles and prophets, Eph. 2. 20, here called 'the twelve apostles of the Lamb', Rev. 21. 14.

It must be borne in mind that the church which is both the body and the bride of Christ was not founded on – or even in part on – the apostle Paul. He came in much later. It was founded on the original twelve spoken of in Acts 1.

Have we here a pictorial setting forth of the 'mystery' of Eph. 3. 18, the dimensions of which are mentioned? In it there is *no inequality*, all come in on the same terms. The precious stones and precious metals all tell of the many glories which have been bestowed upon it, Eph. 3. 10. The whole of it contained the glory of God and that *glory* was enshrined in the Lamb who was its *lamp*-container, see Rev. 21. 23 RV. It did not need the light-bearers of Genesis 1. 14-17. Purity, transparency, beauty characterized this city which everywhere declared the golden glory of God, Rev. 21. 18, 21. It is made up of elements both from land (precious stones) and sea (pearls), from Jews and Gentiles. There was no need for an inner sanctuary, *naos*, for God is not here hidden behind curtains as was the case in the earthly temple, v. 22.

The first five verses of chapter 22 seem to relate to the holy city of chapter 21, and it is a pity that there is a chapter division here. Certain millennial features will doubtless continue into eternity, as verses 3, 4, and 5 imply. Here we have the 'book of life', 'a river of water of life', and 'the tree of fife'. Doubtless in each case life that is life indeed is intended, namely eternal life. Its source is in God. It is not a little remarkable that the Greek word for 'tree' is that which means a dead tree stump, and is so used for that on which the Lord Jesus was impaled. The instrument of death becomes the source of life. The beneficent effects of the cross, 'the leaves of the tree', will be enjoyed by all the nations in the millennium. The effects of the fall are undone and there is no more curse or death.

THE END

REVELATION 22. 6-21

VERSES 6 TO 21 of chapter 22 may be regarded as the grand finish of the Apocalypse. It relates to the Book itself in general, to the Central Person thereof, the Lord Jesus Christ, and to the fact of His soon coming.

Of the *Book* six things are stated: it is 'faithful' in its promises; 'true' in its facts; authoritative in its origin; inevitable as to its foreshadowing; (all in verse 6). It is unsealed, v. 10, and it is complete, vv. 18, 19. There is nothing redundant or lacking, so that none dare take from it or add to it.

As to the central *Person*, He is 'Jesus', v. 16, the name speaking of His humanity and of His sojourn here on earth. He is also 'the root and the offspring of David', v. 16, implying both His deity and humanity. For as the root He was prior to David, and as the offspring He came after him. Further, He is the 'bright and morning star' which shines in the night, before the sun rising, and as such is the Hope of the church. He is the Alpha and Omega, 'the first and the last', 'the beginning and the end', v. 13, the sum total of all divine revelation and He who is outside of the limits of time.

As to His *coming*, it is three times asserted to be 'quickly', vv. 7, 12, 20, and will be followed by compensation for faithfulness on the part of His servants whilst here. In the first two cases there is no response, doubtless due to the fact that nothing meritorious had really been done. But in the third instance, where no remarks touching the lives and work of the believers are found, there is the joyful response, 'Even so, come, Lord Jesus'.

Meanwhile evil and good go on concurrently and apparently unhindered, pending the coming of the Lord when He will call the evil to a halt and reward the good, v. 12.

As we draw these notes to a close let the reader bear in mind that they are merely *Notes*. Much has been left for his own research and spiritual meditation. Our object will have been achieved if the reader goes back to this inspired section of holy scripture and, possibly helped by these suggestions, discovers for himself the hidden treasures that lie beneath the unexplored surface.